Forever Heartfelt

SPRING OF LOVE
BOOK THREE

VIRGINIA TAYLOR

Copyright © 2024 Virginia Taylor

All rights reserved. No part of this publication may be reproduced, distributed or transmitted in any form or by any means, without prior written permission.

Publisher's Note: This is a work of fiction. Names, characters, places, and incidents are a product of the author's imagination. Locales and public names are sometimes used for atmospheric purposes. Any resemblance to actual people, living or dead, or to businesses, companies, events, institutions, or locales is completely coincidental.

Serenade Publishing

www.serenadepublishing.com

Also by Virginia Taylor

Spring of Love Series

Forever Delighted

Forever Amused

Forever Heartfelt

Chapter One

The creaking of the floorboards in the hallway warned Cassia Lacey to stop staring at herself in the long mirror. She quickly shoved her feet into her red velvet evening shoes, and hastened toward the door. "I'm almost ready," she said as she pulled the door open to her pretty stepmother. "You look so elegant, Nora." Her voice tailed off.

"Thank you, my dear," Nora, Lady Lacey said as she swished her dark blue silk evening gown into the room. "I am glad to return the compliment. You look very pretty. That lace gown looks lovely on you."

The lace gown probably did look lovely on Cassia, but she didn't look lovely in the lace gown. She hoped the people she met tonight wouldn't have the same opinion. Although she didn't doubt that her gown was pretty, she knew the style was too fussy for her long Nordic frame. Her taste ran to practical gowns that she could wear comfortably, but the dressmaker in her local village had skimmed through a few pictures and suggested that a plain white slip could be overlaid with organza and trimmed with lace. At the time, this had sounded reasonable.

The gown that had eventuated after that conversation was an enormous sea of organza and lace, and a wave of fabric flowing behind her. Trying to control her panic, she managed to squeeze out an optimistic smile. "Indeed. And if I should need to catch butterflies, these sleeves would be useful."

Nora's smile wavered. "The lace cost your father a small fortune. But, perhaps your hair..." She gaze fixed on the ringlets that had been gathered on each side of Cassia's head, some already drooping to her bare shoulders.

Cassia swung around to face the mirror. "I know. The curl won't hold. It never does. This style is Hobson's idea, not mine. It's the latest fashion, Hobson said." Hobson, the maid hired with the town house had recommended herself as a good hair stylist, and had also said the hairstyle suited Cassia. The style might suit Nora, who had dark, naturally curly locks, but Cassia's hair was thick, dead straight, and pale blonde. Styling a simple knot took seconds, but town-bred Hobson thought that having a first season in London called for a hairdo that wasted at least an hour, or more, if anyone had bothered to count the rag-rolling beforehand.

"Perhaps you need a few more pins." Shifting the sparse skirts of her turquoise silk gown past the corner of the four-poster bed, Nora made her way through the tiny bedroom to Cassia's side. "I thought curls would suit you, but perhaps... oh, dear, your poor father has been waiting so patiently. I would rather not hold him up any longer."

"Of course not." In the most tactful way, she had told Cassia exactly what she, Cassia, thought – that her hair looked best simply styled. "You go down and I'll be there in three minutes, or we will have Papa tapping his foot and trying to think of an excuse not to go."

"Sir Robert does so dislike being in the city. A month, I told him. We've only been here for two days and already he's fretting about the fruit." Nora spun around and hastened away, leaving only the rustle of silk in her wake.

Cassia ruthlessly tore out her pins and dragged her brush through her hair. Despite the fashion for elaborate hairstyles, she preferred to keep hers sleek. The shape of her face, almost rectangular with high cheekbones and a wide mouth, tended to look horsey at the best of times. Adding bunches of ringlets to the sides didn't help.

In a few seconds she had scraped her hair to the top of her head and begun a thick plait. She twirled the length into a cone and pushed her pins firmly into place. After a moment's consideration, she separated out a thin lock of hair on either side of her face, hoping that a finer strand might keep the curl for the next few hours. She would have been delighted to rip the elaborate lace off her gown, too, having only agreed to the addition to please her stepmother. Nora had been captured by the idea of having a stepdaughter to introduce into society and had assumed that the more money she spent, the better the garment.

After clipping on her pearl necklace, which had once belonged to her mother, Cassia snatched up her pink and white striped shawl and matching reticule, and hurried down the stairs. She had resigned herself to wasting the next month on the marriage market.

"Young Mr. Penrose is wasting far too much time sewing

his wild oats," Papa had muttered. *"It's time he realized the happiness he was missing."*

Last year, Cassia had seen no need to contribute to George Penrose's happiness. Although she fully expected to marry George, her dearest love since childhood and a neighbor in the country, she was content to wait until he was ready to settle down—or so she had thought until last year when Nora and her two young sons had joined the household. This year, a red-faced, colicky infant had been added to the mix, and chaos had erupted.

Although she tried her best to embrace this new family of hers, the idea of a London season didn't seem as mindless as she previously thought. Therefore, she finally conceded to her father's hopes for her. Apparently, the sight of her dressed in frills and furbelows, meant for sweet young things, would cause George's eyes to light up, and he would be speaking to Papa before he knew where he was. Although she would have liked to stay with one of Papa's cousins, Nora had suggested the hiring of a house for the whole family, meaning that Cassia still hadn't found her peaceful haven.

Acting swiftly on his wife's suggestion, Papa had counted himself lucky to have been put in contact with a gentleman who had decided to tour the continent with his large family. This meant that the Lacey contingent, which now consisted of three adults, two active little boys, one noisy baby and his righteous nanny, now occupied a furnished house staffed with servants who ran the establishment as efficiently as any house full of disruptions could be run.

This morning the boys had awoken just after dawn and

had been playing pirates, 'ahoy-ing' the frazzled servants from the upper landing. Even now, from the bottom of the staircase, she could hear noisy thundering back and forth, and doors slamming as they disputed with the nursery maid about the proper time to go to bed.

She stopped at the bottom of the staircase, took a deep breath, smoothed her hair, and walked with assumed calm into the blue-papered sitting room at the front of the house.

"Well, well," Papa said smiling from his position in front of the black marble fireplace. "The time taken was worth the effort, eh?" Handsome and distinguished in his white cravat and carefully tailored black jacket, Papa turned to Nora, his eyebrows lifted. At fifty, although his fair hair had begun to gray at the temples, he still had the tall upright posture of a younger man, possibly because he remained actively involved in the running of his country estate.

"Oh, Cassia." Nora glanced doubtfully at Cassia's feet. "Red shoes? Do you think ...?"

Cassia's chest deflated. "These are my comfortable dancing slippers. I'm sure no one will notice them."

"You looked delightful, my dear," Papa said in his gentle voice. He always said that. Although she was still his pride and joy, he hadn't objected to bringing his only daughter to town so that she could grab herself a marriage proposal.

She smiled. "Thank you, Papa." She always said that, too, though she felt more comfortable in plain styles. "Presumably the carriage awaits?"

"Indeed." He held out a hand to Nora who had moved

to his side. "Time to leave, Lady Lacey. Do not forget to save a dance for me."

"They're all for you, Sir Robert." Nora slid her hand under his arm. Her paisley shawl drooped fashionably from one white shoulder to one gloved elbow.

Cassia turned away. With a conscious smile, she preceded the couple to the front door, which the elderly footman hastened to open. She thanked him and breathed in the night air. A million stars twinkled in the clear black sky, heralding perfect weather for at least tomorrow. Late spring, the temperatures varied from day to day.

Unfortunately, she would be missing the perfect time to be at home working with the gardener on her new plantings. Although Nora managed the house, she had no interest in the outdoor area, leaving Cassia to continue with her design for the acre surrounding the sprawling Tudor manor house built by her ancestors. The rolling green lawn with a fountain in the center had been finished recently but Cassia's dreams had expanded at the same rate as her father's modest income. Last year, she had added a cartwheel rim of formal hedges, which had been sectioned to frame perennials, a style that suited the old house. She longed to be home.

This next month would be a shocking waste of her precious time. Mindful of her skirts, she climbed into the carriage, trying to concentrate on the task ahead, determined to smile at all good marriage prospects, without appearing at all approachable.

The noble Adam Robert James Huntley, Duke of Huntsdale, Earl of Chilton and Baron Huntley, lifted his chin as he carefully knotted his starched cravat. Fingering the creases into place, he examined his reflection in the mirror.

Last year he had ignored the ball season. He had ignored the season the year before. Nothing interested him less than debutantes. In the six years since his father's death, he had hired and fired staff, made new friends and enemies, and ignored balls. He didn't need a wife, not then. Two months ago, he had met his perfect duchess and changed his mind.

After his valet gave Huntsdale's evening jacket one last swipe with the brush, Adam collected his hat and his white gloves, and strolled to the drawing room to await his younger brother, Jake Everley, who had recently come down from Oxford. Tonight would be his first experience of the London ball season.

"You take as long as a girl to get ready." Grinning, Jeremy straightened out from his sprawled position on the faded brocade couch by the window that faced Grosvenor Square.

With all the heavy Huntsdale furniture, handed down over the years, as well as a few ornaments his mother had chosen, furnished the room. Huntsdale could never decide if his house looked interesting or overcrowded. Too much of everything had been the fashion when his parents were young. They had spared no expense in the building of this new town house. This part of his inheritance was large enough for a family of ten, and crowded with dust catchers.

Eying his brother, Huntsdale said, "If you won't take

the time to hire yourself a valet, please make use of mine. For now, let me see what I can do with that dish-wipe you are using as a cravat." He stood shoulder to shoulder with the now twenty-two year-old, each the same height, six feet and two inches, the same weight, and similar dark hair and light eyes. Jeremy had a milder expression than Huntsdale, or so their parents had said, and a less competitive edge. "There. I hope you have taken note."

"I couldn't unless I had eyes planted beneath my chin. If you have finished fussing over me, may we leave?"

"Is the carriage at the door?"

"Awaiting your grace. I promised not to be late. Cornelia wants to be sure of a partner for the first dance." Jeremy referred to Cornelia Gerard, whose family's house had been built near the Huntsdale estate in Kent. Jeremy and Cornelia saw each other as family, though Huntsdale suspected Cornelia had a yen for his even-tempered brother.

"Don't turn her head with your attentions."

Jeremy bridled. "She doesn't see me *that way*. Nor I, her. It wouldn't be right, not when I think of all I owe her family. Aside from that, I'm planning to get myself a mistress."

Huntsdale stood stock still, his posture rigid. "You are *what*?"

"His grace had a talk to me when I was about sixteen. He told me to stay away from what he termed *women of the night*. A man needs a woman and I don't meet many who don't expect marriage first. And you have one."

Strictly speaking, the phrase 'you have one' should have been 'you *had* one,' but Huntsdale had no intention of discussing the matter with his younger brother. However, about a month ago, Huntsdale had dismissed the mistress he'd had for the past four years, leaving her with an income, the house she currently occupied, and the use of the carriage that came with their original agreement until she accepted her next project. "*Find someone clean and tidy who is willing to let you visit her two or three times a week in exchange for a small house and a goodly allowance.* Yes, my lord duke said the same to me, but I didn't snatch up the first woman I saw at the age of twenty-two."

"You were still at Oxford."

"You are barely down yourself." When his parents had died, Huntsdale had still been living in his Oxford rooms. After the funeral, he had discovered that the estate books had been left in a mess. The former Duke of Huntsdale had not expected to contract a fever at the age of forty-eight and pass the infection to his wife. The former Earl of Chiltern. Adam, subsequently became the duke and began to learn the ins and outs of his inheritance. Jeremy had been left with a reasonable income, and a bequest from his maternal grandfather gave him a neat little country property. He largely ignored both, which didn't matter to Huntsdale who thought his brother should have the leisure to live the life he had wanted for himself at that same age.

He followed Jeremy into the vast marbled hallway. The footman swung open the front door and Huntsdale let his impatient brother precede him into the dusk. Clouds shrouded the darkening sky as he climbed into the carriage.

Barely ten minutes later, his driver left him and his brother at the front of Burleigh House, where the ball would be held. After a trudge up the outside steps, he waited in line with Jeremy to be received by his hosts. From there, he proceeded into the ballroom where a magnificent crystal chandelier dominated the high-domed ceiling. The area glittered with the light from hundreds of candles, which reflected on the three sets of mullioned windows.

Jeremy scanned the room, indicating a group of people chatting near the gilded fireplace. "I see Cornelia. Coming over?"

Spotting Mr. Bertram Gerard, one of his cronies, Huntsdale strolled toward the group comprising Sir Waldo and Lady Gerard and an assortment of young ladies dressed in white gowns. Huntsdale nodded and greeted each curtsey with a bow as he was introduced by Lady Gerard. Finally he moved off with Bertie, who had been at Oxford with him, as had many of the lads from Eton. "Roped in, I see."

Bertie offered a guileless smile. "I don't mind attending these affairs. Have to, as it happens, but it's not all bad. I am expected to dance with my sister's friends." Clearly satisfied with the situation, he lifted two eyebrows, and glanced across at Miss Essie Deering, a pretty dark-haired female dainty enough to suit a man barely five feet and nine inches tall. Miss Deering lowered her gaze demurely. Huntsdale suspected his friend was in with a chance, if he wanted her.

After a brief glance at the other young ladies, each of whom pretended not to notice, Huntsdale scanned the rest of the room, not spotting the woman he hoped to see. "The pup's thinking of taking a mistress," he said idly, crossing his arms and leaning back.

Bertie raised his eyebrows. "Family tradition, eh?"

"He's too young for that sort of commitment." Huntsdale frowned. "My case was entirely different. I didn't have time to go gallivanting around with the rest of you. He does."

"He certainly doesn't have your responsibilities. And he's a peaceful kind of chap, not one like you who needs a spot of—let's say—calming down. Mrs. Smith has done wonders for you. Civilized you in a way."

Huntsdale didn't bother telling Bertie, either, that Mellie was no longer in his life. But she *had* civilized him. Two years older than his twenty-eight, she had taught him how to please a woman, physically. She had taught him that he couldn't always have the last word. She had taught him that losing his temper didn't win arguments. He already knew that bullying a woman would never change her mind, for he had learned this first essential from his parents, whose arguments raged on for days and usually ended in his father marching out of the house and his mother weeping noisily. The sound of a woman crying still turned his blood to water. He had never made Mellie cry, but she didn't love him. He didn't love her either, and if truth be told, he hadn't thought of her at all this past month. "That's a high compliment to her, and a low blow for me."

"Sorry, old chap, but it's the truth."

Huntsdale nodded, but of course he hadn't chosen to keep a mistress because he needed calming down. That had been purely incidental. He had found out not long after succeeding to the title that the life of a young man who had inherited a fortune was not the same as a young earl with expectations. His parents' death had left him with huge responsibilities to an expanding workforce.

The power of his money also influenced the wives and

sisters and daughters of the men with whom he was acquainted. If he spotted an interesting woman, he could never be sure if she liked him or if she was calculating the time he would take to open his purse—or if she wanted a certain advancement for her man, or even if she had been put in his path for either of those reasons. He had grown cynical quickly. Had he accepted the sexual favors from a fraction of the women who offered, he would be a marked man. Better to be known as a fellow satisfied by his own woman.

Lady Gerard, apparently unable to tolerate the sight of two eligible males standing together companionably, cajoled him into dancing with a young lady who stared at his shirtfront during the entire dance. He tried idle chitchat, with no success. He was too tall, she was too short, he was too experienced, and she was too innocent. He thanked her as he led her off the floor—thanked her for giving him a proper chance to spot the reason why he had attended the ball tonight.

He had seen Her, standing in a corner with her father and a shorter woman in dark blue overpowered by a bunch of curls sprouting on either side of head. As his gaze left the female he presumed to be her chaperone, Miss Lacey glanced at him and away. He frowned. Yet again she hadn't acknowledged him. The last time she had done this, he had made the effort to reintroduce himself. This time she could only be deliberately ignoring him. He had no idea why.

From the moment he first met her, he had enjoyed her candid comments, which few young ladies offered him. He had watched her try not to take over when she could clearly organize any function more efficiently than had been done, and he appreciated that she had no idea how she looked. She was the most atrociously dressed woman he had met, and likely the most beautiful without her clothes, which he carefully tried not to imagine in public, and even now failed. The latter he would very much like to find out, first hand.

Pondering his tactics, he moved not too far out of her vicinity. On the way to the cards' room he saw two friends, the first of whom was George Penrose, a friend since Eton. A week ago, George had mentioned Miss Lacey would be here tonight, which had caused Huntsdale to drop a previous commitment and accept the invitation to be present. As a youngster, Penrose had plighted his troth to Miss Lacey, a story that amused him these days. Huntsdale didn't know if he should seriously consider this promise when George certainly didn't.

First he greeted redheaded Lord Lucien Walton, who had also attended Oxford with him, and then he turned to George. "Been here long?"

"Unexpectedly detained." Penrose winked. Although his family, who owned a good deal of Surrey, occupied themselves in the country, he currently lived in the Penrose town house, banished from home for a misdemeanor, rumor said. This hadn't inconvenienced him at all. "Have you seen Cassia? I'm supposed to dance with her tonight."

Huntsdale feigned a wrinkle in his glove. "Cassia?"

"Miss Lacey. My friend from the country. You met her in Surrey. Twice."

Huntsdale pretended to consider. "The dark-haired housemaid?"

"A lady. White hair. Well, blonde hair."

Huntsdale raised his gaze and saw the aforementioned approach, followed by the woman he tardily recognized as her stepmother. Miss Lacey ignored Huntsdale and turned her flashing smile on Penrose, the lucky dog, while Huntsdale stood dry-mouthed and trying not to fidget. "You're late. We've been watching for you, haven't we, Nora?"

"You have been very much in demand on the dance floor, Cassia," Lady Lacey said firmly. "You certainly have not been watching for Mr. Penrose."

"May I recall my friend, the Duke of Huntsdale to you, Cassia? And, of course, Lord Walton."

The blonde glanced at him in query. A hundred matchmaking mothers knew his name without ever meeting him, and this woman, whom he had met twice, insisted she never remembered that fact, or his face, or even his name. Yet again, she looked blank. Disappointment deflated his chest.

He politely tilted his eyebrows. "I'm not sure ..."

Her face expressed doubt. "Have we indeed met before?"

He shook his head, desperately trying to appear equally puzzled. "Perhaps at the Lenton's ball?" He hadn't attended that.

She shook her head. "Perhaps at George's picnic? I rarely leave Surrey. Please forgive my wretched memory." Her white-gloved hand extended. "Since George forgot to introduce my step-mama, Lady Lacey, I shall do so." She indicated the other woman.

Huntsdale bowed politely. His glance lingered on Miss Lacey's gown. The appalling concoction appeared to have been made out of every scrap of expensive fabric in England. The enormous sleeves alone could have been tossed over a supper table and used to keep the blundering moths off the food. Knowing he had to treat her as coolly as she treated him, he lifted his gaze to her beautiful, icy blue eyes. "Two *Lacey* women."

A spot of color warmed her cheeks. "Thank you for noticing."

He shrugged, knowing that whatever he said would make no difference to her. His title didn't impress her and, other than his money, he had little else to recommend him. He may as well continue as he started, as a persistent man without a scrap of George's outgoing personality.

"Lacey. Lacy gown." Lady Lacey smiled. "Oh, that's so clever, your grace. I never would have thought of that when I chose the gown."

"So, she has you to thank?"

Miss Lacey turned her back on him. "George, I've put you on my card for this dance." She latched onto Penrose's arm, and dragged him into the swirl of people.

Tightening his jaw, Huntsdale bowed to Lady Lacey. "May I have the honor of this dance?"

She took a step back, clearly astonished. "Oh, indeed, I would be delighted."

He offered his arm and led her to the floor, where he let himself be arranged into a group for a country-dance. Older than his last partner, she didn't need to watch her feet and managed to speak to him while performing in the energetic romp. During the course of the exercise, he plotted his next maneuver. Long ago, he had applied himself to dancing lessons for a purpose, and that purpose had been to hold females in his arms.

After he escorted Lady Lacey back to her equally

pleasant husband, he remained conversing politely with the couple, awaiting Miss Lacey. He would not allow her to escape him again. This might possibly be his last chance tonight to add his name to her list of possibles, which he suspected would fill quickly.

Miss Lacey arrived back laughing and out of breath. The moment she spotted him, her expression changed to polite indifference. Before she could step out of his path, he indicated the dance floor. "May I have the pleasure of being your next partner?"

"Of course you may," Penrose said, smiling down at her. "She has to dance with my friends. I told her she would meet you all. You dance this next with her and I'll line up Lucien and Bertie. Who else is here?"

Huntsdale shrugged. "Jeremy? Other than that, just the usual crowd." He turned to Miss Lacey whose red velvet shoe tapped impatiently. "This next is a cotillion. Will that suit you?"

"Certainly, your grace." Her expression resigned, she rested the tips of her fingers on his arm.

His mind filled with frustrating thoughts. Each time they met during the dance, he smiled at her, until finally she managed to smile back. "That's better," he said. "I don't remember why we fell out. Do you?"

"Did we argue?" The dance took her to the other end of the room.

"I thought we got on rather well," he said as he grabbed at her hand to race with her under an avenue of arms. She glanced at him but she didn't answer until they stood face-to-face, ready to sashay toward each other.

"I'm afraid I don't remember," ended the circle of questions so neatly that he could only smile. At least she spoke civilly now and had relaxed a little. Next time they met she might deign to use his name.

The strict rules of etiquette forbade him to dance with the same lady more than twice. So that he hadn't singled Miss Lacey out for attention, he danced with Bertie's sister, his mother, and finally his hostess. Having achieved his main purpose, he could leave. He searched out Jeremy, whom he finally found in a corner of the ballroom with Lucien and Bertie. All were scanning the dancers with a collective connoisseurs' eye. "Spot anyone interesting?" he asked Jeremy.

"Half of them are female, therefore half of them are interesting. I'm just deciding whom I'll ask to dance next."

"I'm leaving now. Bertie, could you drop Jeremy off? You live the closest to us."

"You can't go yet," Lucien said, frowning. "You've hardly danced with anyone except married ladies."

"Married ladies don't expect me to offer for them. Aside from that, I danced with Bertie's sister, Corinne, and her friend." Huntsdale left Miss Lacey off his list, not about to call attention to her.

"Don't let the team down. It's our duty, no matter how tedious, to make sure that sweet young ladies are whirled all around the room. We should make their first formal outing an occasion to remember, not a night to forget." Lucien smoothed the backs of his white gloves.

Huntsdale narrowed his eyes. "I must be mistaken. For a moment I thought you were Lucien Walton."

"Well, it's only manners, old chap. Or to be more truthful, Lady Gerard. She gave me a lecture, the bones of which

I have repeated to you, but it's no hardship, not really. Some of the sweet young things are having the night of their lives and it's rather pleasant to be wrapped in their enthusiasm. Contribute, Adam. It won't do you any harm. Aside from that, then the few ladies you did honor with a dance won't think more of your gesture than you meant."

Huntsdale only needed to ponder for few minutes before deciding Lucien was right. He shouldn't openly pursue Cassia. A well-dowered, secure woman, she needed neither money nor position. She needed to be intrigued and certain she had chosen her own path.

Chapter Two

"His Grace of Huntsdale is a very interesting gentleman."

Cassia stared at Nora in surprise while the carriage carefully took the corner. Her feet ached, but she had been impressed by George's friends, most of whom she could describe as very pleasant. The duke, or Huntsdale as his friends called him, was rather more of a puzzle, though the words *persistent* or even *annoying* came to mind. "Yes," she said to Nora because to disagree would mean explaining herself, and she didn't want to talk about the autocratic dilettante. "Though perhaps a little too ..."

"Too what?"

"I can't quite say."

"Perfect?" her father contributed.

"I would *never* call him perfect," Cassia said, slightly affronted. "Not when the man has scandalized society for the past few years with his light women."

"Light women?" Nora turned to raise her eyebrows at

Papa. "I hadn't heard that he wasted his time in dalliances. He seems to have a spotless reputation, despite the fact that he's so attractive. I'm sure your father doesn't mind me noticing that the duke is handsome when he is much closer to you in age than to me."

Papa leaned forward in his seat to take his wife's hand. "I forbid you to notice handsome men." His tone sounded low and intimate.

Nora giggled.

Cassia tried not to notice.

Her father turned his attention back to Cassia. "And exactly how has the duke scandalized society?"

"I don't think we should discuss the matter." She shuffled her shoulders into the upholstery.

"But apparently you already have, or you wouldn't know that he has scandalized society."

"I haven't discussed a thing." Cassia said, trying to avoid being petulant. "I've listened to George's tales."

"Not a sound idea, I would have thought. George needs to look to his own behavior before discrediting others."

"I expect we all do, but George is my friend and, therefore, I trust him." A chink in the carriage window blew the cool night air across her shoulders. She shifted her shawl to cover the back of her neck. "He knows he can say anything to me, and he warned me about the duke. After I met him, I saw why."

"Huntsdale behaved in a courteous manner tonight. He introduced himself to your family before he asked you to dance with him."

"I don't mean tonight." She stared at Papa. "Tonight, he was apparently on his best behavior. I'm sure you remember George organizing a picnic for his town friends in Surrey last month. I met the duke then. You were too busy to come, but Nora would remember because she also attended with Tommy and Frankie."

Nora nodded. "I was introduced to him that day, but Mrs. Penrose organized the tables so that all the young people sat together. I sat with the parents, so that we could keep an eye on our children. You said you had a delightful day, Cassia. I certainly did and the boys enjoyed themselves immensely, because of the pony rides and the games and the sweet treats."

"The weather was nice, the day was perfectly organized, and *some* of the company was delightful."

"I imagine you are singling out Huntsdale with that word *some*." Papa tugged at his shirt cuffs. "I am interested now to know how a duke offended my only daughter the first time he met her."

"I didn't say he was offensive. He is polished without being smooth. He couldn't have been more polite to me had I been the queen." She glanced at the lit windows in the street as the carriage began to slow, hoping she sounded suitably diffident, though she doubted anyone in the world could be diffident about Huntsdale.

The first sight of him would take any woman's breath. Not only was he slightly taller than the other gentlemen, he had powerful shoulders, a lean torso, and long muscular legs. She, a country girl with little experience of men, had been left wordless when he had focused his eyes of cornflower blue on her. His smile, the dazzling whiteness, his utter confidence, had turned her head and she had melted.

"Do walk with me, George's Cassia," he had said, and he

had hoisted his picnic basket onto his shoulder without the slightest effort and led her to the long table in the midst of a stand of shady elm trees. A group of other young people followed with more baskets, trailed by parents or chaperones. The table placements had been pre-arranged. She already knew she would be sitting beside George.

In all, Cassia wouldn't call Huntsdale loquacious. He was more a doer than a thinker, but a woman couldn't complain when that worked in her favor. Being a duke, because he wanted a particular seat, he took the particular seat, which left him sitting on her right, and extremely flattered. While George quite properly attended to the young lady on his left, Huntsdale served Cassia with all the delicacies he had brought with him from town, and he kept her glass fresh with lemonade. He seemed to instinctively know what she might be lacking. Not only that, but he engaged her in more than one interesting subject. She decided the handsome visitor from London was quite marvelous.

"I had a very pleasant chat with his grace tonight." Her father shifted from his position on the middle of the forward seat to the door, as the carriage prepared to stop. The hired house had been sited on the edge of a park, within walking distance of the main thoroughfares. "The man is certainly approachable."

She glanced at him, knowing exactly how Huntsdale had managed to wriggle his way into Papa's good books. Papa wasn't the type of man to be impressed by a title. He preferred plain speaking and good manners, and Huntsdale was an expert at faking both.

Papa lifted his shoulders. "He was the only one of

George's friends who took the trouble to engage me in intelligent conversation."

"That's a habit of his," Cassia said, her chin raised. "He likes to impress his inferiors."

"Cassia, if you know something about him that I should know, please say so." The carriage pulled to a halt.

"Everyone knows. He is having a relationship with a woman."

Papa pushed the door open. "Is the man not allowed to have relationships with women?"

She watched him step out of the carriage while sifting through her words. "We have no need to cozy up to him," she said, her voice low, as Nora stood, preparing to leave. "He is not on the marriage market. He keeps a mistress."

Papa stared at her, frowning, and grasped Nora's hand while she used the shaky step. "It's not uncommon, Cassia, though that hardly makes him comfortably placed. Did you know, Nora?"

"I don't know any of the town gossip, though at the picnic I sat beside Lady Gerard, who tried to catch me up. But naturally, she wouldn't tell me about a duke's mistress."

"I'm very lucky that George warned me." Her posture erect, Cassia stepped out of the carriage. "Otherwise I might have had my head turned."

Nora took her arm, gazing at her with sympathy. "I can understand your disillusionment, but as your papa says, it is not uncommon for a man to take a mistress."

"Perhaps I should be glad to hear that at last reality has entered into my sheltered daughter's life," Papa said with a strange glance at her.

"After I heard about his paid woman, my conversation

with the duke diminished greatly, as you might imagine." Head lowered, Cassia trudged arm in arm with Nora to the door, with Papa behind while the driver moved off, heading into the laneway that led to the carriage house.

Papa used the door-knocker. At home, the butler would be waiting and open the door as soon as he heard the carriage. "What can I say other than a man who has a mistress tends not to tumble the housemaids and leave them with very noisy bundles to care for?" A housemaid opened the door and stood aside.

"One of our royal dukes lived with his mistress and no one turned a hair." Nora walked through into the cramped hallway.

Cassia followed behind her. "That was in the olden days, before he married."

"He had historical precedence," Papa said, as the maid handed him a single oil lamp. "The mistresses of kings had very important positions. Since Huntsdale is a duke and decidedly rich, we can forgive him."

"No," Cassia said, her throat inexplicably constricted. "He's a duke and no friend of mine. Now, I'm going up to bed." With that, she took the stairs in a rush, wanting to get to her tiny room before she looked even more foolish.

Reality had indeed entered her life. When she had met Huntsdale, she hadn't seen him as duke, but as a wildly attractive, single male. Until that point she had assumed she loved George, but George had never left her breathless. She didn't tingle when he touched her. Whereas, the barest touch of Huntsdale's fingers had paralyzed her. She couldn't move, couldn't breathe, couldn't think, and she could barely take her gaze from him. She could have sworn he was equally attracted.

Then George had nudged her, and said close to her ear, "Watch out for Huntsdale."

"Watch out?"

George smiled mysteriously. "He's a little too experienced for you."

"I don't know what you mean," she said under her breath.

"You won't turn his head, you know. He has a very beautiful mistress."

She had stared straight ahead. He had a beautiful mistress. The words sank in her chest and flushed her cheeks. She had been foolish to think he treated her with more than courtesy. Naturally, when a friend of a friend began to flirt with him, as a duke, he had the manners to handle her without a cut direct. An aristocrat lived in a rarified atmosphere, one in which, as the daughter of a mere knight, she didn't belong. That day, the duke merely acted as any normal male would, accepting her admiration with courtesy. Her breathless voice, her long gazes, her rackety breathing were hers alone, and not due to any equal admiration from him.

She had pressed her hands against her cheeks, cooling her hot embarrassment. How childish she had been to imagine he found her attractive. Likely, his smiles came from his grown-up thoughts about his mistress's curvaceous body, and his hopes that time would pass quickly until he saw her again. He would instantly forget about the callow country spinster who had eaten his every word. Much to her shame, while she had been laughing with him, and wallowing in his attention, she had completely forgotten about George. Within a week, the duke would be accepting ragging from his friends about turning the head of a country mouse.

Fortunately, picnics were not formal affairs and he was forced to move soon after. After that embarrassing day, she'd had the opportunity to treat him as any other forgettable acquaintance, with a brief nod or faked blindness, which she practiced within the next week at a wedding in Kent. She nodded formally and disappeared, but he found her and re-introduced himself.

Tonight, she hadn't wanted to speak to him at all, but his ducal manners made rags of her intentions. Apparently, she had no choice other than to speak to him on any occasion he decided to recognize her. If so, she needed to take rigid control of her reactions.

Fortunately, a lamp had been left burning in her room. She pulled the pins out of her hair and dropped them onto the flower-painted dish on the dressing table. Left without a maid of her own, and after almost turning her arms inside out, she managed to untie her gown. A tap on her door stopped her stepping out of the garment.

"Cassia. Do you need help disrobing?"

"I've managed, thank you, Nora."

"May I speak to you for a moment?"

Cassia didn't want to talk to Nora. She wanted to hold her palms over her hot cheeks and reason with herself. She wanted to scrub tonight out of her brain. She wanted to start again and make herself more clear to George, who would be a suitable match for her. Instead, she flicked back her plait and straightened her shoulders. "Indeed you may. Come in."

"We could talk in the morning if you would rather." The flickering light from Nora's candle appeared, then the rest of her. "But Lady Gerard introduced me to Lady Sheldon, who I am sure you know is a famous hostess." She drew a deep breath. "I assume she was impressed that you were one of the few that the duke asked to dance because she invited us to her supper dance. Naturally I couldn't refuse because it is a great honor, but I didn't like to mention it in front of your father in case you don't like the idea."

"We weren't planning on making a great splash, Nora. Lord Burleigh is an old friend of Papa's but other than George's friends, we hardly know anyone else."

"One of George Penrose's friends is a duke. We now know more people than we expected. Lady Gerard has also decided to take us up. In fact, she had an idea that I would like to put to you."

Cassia sat on the bed and indicated the plush dressing stool to Nora, who left her candle burning on the dressing table where the reflection cast in the three oval mirrors expanded the light of the lamp fourfold. "Go ahead."

Nora's gaze met hers. "We hadn't thought we might be admitted to high society events when we made our plans for you. We thought we would fill the month with the Burleigh's ball and a few functions held by connections of your father. Sir Robert didn't want to stay any longer than that."

"Nor do I. I want to get back to my garden." Cassia picked at the quilted satin counterpane on the bed.

"Your future is at stake, Cassia. You need to take the subject of marriage seriously."

Cassia smiled, slightly baffled. "I thought I was here to hurry George along. He is already introducing me to his town friends. I'm sure they all suspect I am promised to him."

Nora dropped her gaze. "I'm not sure *he* knows that you consider yourself promised to him. If so, he needs to discover that if he doesn't snap you up soon, he will lose his chance. Nothing spurs a man like competition." She moistened her lips. "Lady Gerard suggested that I might like to alternate chaperonage with her. She has one daughter to present and so do I. If I take her daughter with us, and she takes you with hers, neither of us need go out night after night. She has another two daughters at home. And she can introduce you to the other society hostesses, which I can't, not knowing anyone of importance in town."

"Do you really think that if I attend more functions that George will attempt to snap me up before anyone else does?"

"There's no harm in trying. Friday night will see the next ball of the season. Lady Gerard means to take her daughter, Cornelia, and Essie Deering, and she said she can manage an invitation for you as well, should you wish to join them."

"I have no great objection." Cassia hadn't minded George being sure of her before, but last year she had lived with Papa in a peaceful, childless household that she ran her own way. Although she hadn't planned to marry until she was so old she saw no other choice, her choices had been taken from her by two bouncy little step-brothers and a sweet, but very demanding baby.

"Then on Wednesday night, Mrs. Deering would do the honors. I said if we went to the assembly rooms, I could chaperone next week, with Jane Matthew's mother. Lady Gerard thought two chaperones each time would be plenty. We would have a covey of six young ladies. You are the sixth."

Cassia's mouth dried. She would have five young ladies to tower over, five young ladies to whom she would need to explain her unmarried state. However, when she married, her restlessness, and uncertainly of her place in the Lacey household since the birth of her half-brother, would be relieved. "But do you think my wardrobe will stand it?" she said, experiencing a glimmer of hope.

"You won't regret this for one minute, darling Cassia. The more people you meet, the more competition for George. He still thinks of you as a friend. You might open his eyes to your value when he sees other men admiring you. I can't believe this wonderful opportunity has tumbled right into our laps." Nora reached out and took Cassia's hands. "No one knows better than I how hard it is to find a husband when the first blush of youth has left. I had been on my own for five years before I found your father and there he was, tall and handsome and looking at me as if I were nineteen all over again." Her pretty lips trembled with earnestness.

Cassia smiled wryly. "I think he had the same reaction. I'm glad you found each other." She didn't doubt for a moment that her father had made a love match.

Nora had been married to Papa's lawyer, who had died unexpectedly. She had gone to live with her sister and only on rare occasions visited the local library. Papa had been delighted when he saw her outside and they had married within a few months. The honeymoon had barely finished when her belly had begun to swell. The pregnancy hadn't been easy, and she had needed to put her feet up, which meant that she couldn't be expected to run the household. Cassia had managed nicely by herself. Then baby Jack was born.

After that, Nora had assumed the full responsibility of a role she hadn't enlarged year-by-year as Cassia had. Although the older woman possessed a good heart, every single change she made diminished Cassia in her own eyes. Soon the only memories of her mother would be her own.

She drew in a deep breath. Times without number, middle-class Nora had peered out of her comfortable world. Despite wanting nothing more than to run back to hers, Cassia should equal the other woman's temerity. "We could call on Lady Gerard tomorrow."

"Perhaps we should have done so before." Nora said, her expression guilty. "She and I had a most enjoyable gossip at the picnic in Surrey but I hesitated to be pushy. She much admired your gown tonight, Cassia."

"That's very gratifying." Cassia hoped Nora had told Lady Gerard who had chosen the style, but that would be too much to wish for. "I have to say I don't know her daughter Cornelia at all well, but it would be nice to have someone with whom to share the, hmm, pleasure of a ball season." Knowing she had little in common with the young lady, she willed herself to mean what she said.

Nora rose to her feet, a relieved smile on her face. "I must make an early start in the morning. I want to show Tommy and Frankie the sights, and afterward your father has a few people he wants me to meet, too." After planting a quick kiss on Cassia's cheek, Nora left the room, closing the door carefully behind her.

Cassia stayed sitting on her bed, her eyes on her comfortable red velvet shoes, her mind everywhere else. Her father had *a few people he wanted Nora to meet*. Her father used to have a few people he wanted Cassia to meet. She chewed at her lip. Papa had no need of a daughter now. He had a wife and her two boys, and a new son of his own to inherit his properties. A little more than a year ago, whomever Cassia married would have expected to do so.

Her throat thickened. A spinster daughter was of no use to a father with other calls on his time. Her only use was to marry advantageously. George, as a near neighbor, as a friend, as the heir to his father's lands, had been her logical partner, and as such had been accepted by her father. All her life she had walked along this path, thinking she could marry whenever George cared to give up his single life. Nothing had altered except her reality now that her father and Nora had three young children to bring up. They didn't need Cassia changing Nora's orders, and trying to show Nora how to do each task Cassia's way.

She toed off each of her shoes, which dropped to the floor with a dull thud. Her vision blurred, she slipped out of her gown, unhooked her stays, removed her undergarments, and threw her nightgown over her head. She leaned back against her pillow, her teary eyes closed.

Tomorrow she would attend another ball, and show

George that he ought to propose before someone else did. She needed to be organizing her own household and having her own children.

Chapter Three

Adam's study door opened. He raised his eyebrows at his brother who sauntered into the room and stood in front of the desk. Brought back to a world where the question of land tenancy was unimportant, and a sibling needed backing, Adam dropped his quill onto his blotter. A splotch spread around the nib. "Good afternoon."

His expression wary, Jeremy crossed his arms over his chest, staring down at Adam with resentment. "You asked to see me."

"Indeed I did. You wanted to set up your stables. I heard at the club yesterday that Sandon is selling his stock."

Jeremy pushed out a breath, and dropped his defensive stance by filling his breeches' pockets with his hands. "So, you think I should take a look?"

"I have time today to go with you, if you want me."

"That's kind of you, Adam, but today the Gerards are off to a balloon ascension." Jeremy's face relaxed into a smile. "Bertie wants my company and Cordelia has set up a regular nag about me promising to go with them."

Adam nodded. "Perhaps tomorrow, then."

"Tomorrow will suit me better." Jeremy grinned, turned, and left.

Adam rubbed the back of his neck. From the moment he had inherited his ducal duties, he had grabbed the opportunity to choose his own horses. That his brother didn't feel the same way puzzled him. Although Adam didn't resent in the least the fact that he managed his own interests as well as his brother's, he knew that at some stage the pup needed to take charge of his own life. He was a wealthy young man, who knew nothing about his properties, other than the income they produced. Adding a little responsibility to his agenda would help him grow.

Adam's attention shifted back to the correspondence that his secretary meant him to check. At this time of the year, he would prefer to be overseeing the new building on his country estate, but he had a good manager in his agent, who understood the latest ideas for sturdy foundations. The doorway darkened again.

"Adam?"

He glanced up at George Penrose. "Good afternoon." Leaning back, he set down his pen again. Today he had hoped to catch up with his accounts, but constant interruptions meant that he needed to start each column again. With a wave of his hand, he indicated the leather-upholstered chair on the other side of his desk.

Penrose offered an engaging smile, sauntered into the room and sat, crossing his outstretched legs at the ankle.

The son of a wealthy landowner, he had few worries. He merely needed to know how to entertain himself until he decided which of his father's interests might suit him best. "I made plans to attend the assembly rooms in King Street tonight, but I find I have another commitment. I was hoping you might attend in my place to make up the numbers in the group." He meshed his fingers across his flat belly. A fashionable young blood, fair-haired George wore a burgundy jacket with light tan breeches and boots his valet polished with champagne.

Adam shook his head. "I'll leave the assembly rooms to others. I'm not the sociable type."

George's even featured face expressed his dissatisfaction. "You won't need to be sociable, old chap. You will be part of a large group. Lady Gerard seems to have found no difficulty in having my country friend, Cassia Lacey, approved by the patronesses and is taking her, Cornelia, Essie, and a few others. I heard Mrs. Lacey is chaperoning too."

Adam moistened his throat, hoping he looked hesitant rather than suddenly interested. A man had the rules of polite society to use to his advantage at assembly rooms. She wouldn't refuse to dance with a duke in the presence of her peers. "Since making up the numbers has never concerned you in the least until Miss Lacey arrived in town, should I take it that you have a very particular interest in the lady?"

"Merely a friendly interest. We're from the same area, you know, and we've been friends forever, which you also know. If you are asking if my feelings go any deeper ..." George shrugged. "If in ten years time, I'm not married and nor is she, well, we might consider making a go of it.

Though I'm sure she'll be snapped up long before then. She's clever and nice, and I like her very much, but I can't imagine being in love with her. I've known her since she was a sniveling little brat." He grinned as if he thought Adam might sympathize.

"Sniveling?" Adam curved his mouth into a cynical smile. "She got you into trouble, I'm assuming."

"She did, many times during our lives. But she had a heart of gold and in a brotherly way, I love her."

"Not in a romantic way?"

George frowned. "Why all the questions about me and Cassia?"

"Simple curiosity, that's all."

"Will you go? Lady Gerard can't take a gaggle of females to Almacks without being sure of an equal supply of males. I wouldn't want Cassia standing around for want of a partner, and you danced with her at the Burleigh's ball. I'm sure you can do the same again." George brought his legs back up, as if he had finished with the subject and would leave with or without a favorable answer.

"Yes, I will attend—if I am left enough time this afternoon to finish off the tasks I have planned for today." Adam indicated the pile of papers on his desk.

George grinned and stood. An athlete but never a scholar, he hadn't been at Oxford, but only because his father saw no need when he could teach his son how to manage his expected inheritances. Therefore, George wasn't as close to Adam as Bertie and Lucien. Nevertheless, Adam liked the other chap well enough. Even more, he was pleased to hear that George was not considering marriage with Cassia. Although Adam had no qualms about poaching her, he had never seen George's interest in her to be more than friendly. To have this confirmed satisfied him.

He raced through his accounts, bundled the lot, and walked through into the large adjoining room. "Yes, sir?" His secretary, Cedric Rogers' raised his gaze from the piles of papers on his desk.

"The accounts are satisfactory, and could you cast your eyes over my speech for the House?" Adam indicated the topmost page. He had franked the rest to be posted off.

"I would be happy to do so, my lord." Cedric, blessed with a healthy pair of gray speckled side-whiskers, and a small amount of thinning gray hair, was aged in his late fifties and a whiz with figures. He had formerly been employed by the late duke. "I'm always interested in what you have to say."

"In amongst that pile, I have made a settlement for Mrs. Smith. Her bills are mine for the next six months." Adam moved back to the doorway, mulling over his settlement with Mellie.

The merry widow had inherited a small income and her house after the death of her husband, meaning she didn't rely on Adam for support, but he had enjoyed supplying her with luxuries while they were together. She had filled her home with flowers, and made herself a feminine bower. If she had ever seen his town house, she would have turned up her nose at the interior. Only lately had Adam noticed the stale masculinity of the rooms. These days, perhaps less callow, he preferred the style of Gerard's city home, where the women outnumbered the men, and ornaments were used tastefully, and where conversation overflowed with the light laughter of women.

Memories of his mother filled his heart. Not too long ago, on entering the formal rooms, he would notice wafts of rosemary and lavender. The influence of a woman in his house had now been lost. He no longer noted the gleam on the furniture or the aroma of freshly picked flowers. The most notable aspect in his house these days was the echoing silence. He didn't want the sound of strife back again, but he missed having a female presence in his home. Having one caused a congregation of light voices and laughter. Having none caused a void deeper than loneliness.

Now that he had set mind on Cassia Lacey, he couldn't accept another. Initially her beautiful coloring had attracted him but after engaging her in a meaningful conversation, he found enjoyment in the gleam of humor in her blue eyes, and her inability to agree when she didn't. She didn't bother with 'yes, my lord Duke' where others would, but argued back and forth without worrying about who won or lost while she enjoyed the exercise. Aside from that, no red-blooded male could fight the allure of her graceful body.

"Women like Mrs. Smith make life too easy for a man," Cedric said in his dry, cautious voice. "Best to get yourself locked into matrimony with a female who keeps you on your toes."

Adam smiled somewhat wryly. His mother had certainly kept his father on his toes, and the house echoing with her tantrums. Although her sons had loved her, they hadn't enjoyed the strife and the noisy arguments. Adam wanted a marriage with a woman who knew what she was about, one who could organize his residences without needing his constant input, one who could make intelligent decisions. Cassia Lacey seemed mature and thoughtful, not at all like the impressionable debutants he had met. Aside from that, she was a wholesome country girl with a practical side. Having an interesting face and the sort of body a man wanted to get his hands on was a bonus. "I'm planning to attend the assembly tonight."

"That's the ticket." Cedric didn't raise his head and Adam knew the older man had offered his automatic answer to everything.

Nevertheless, Adam couldn't settle for the rest of the afternoon. At the assembly rooms, he would have more chances to either dance with or talk to Cassia.

And for a man with a mission, this suited him perfectly.

Cassia stared out of the carriage window, pasting a smile on her face to hide the fact that for the first time in her life, she was nervous about attending a function. At home where she knew everyone, her gowns didn't need to be at all fashionable. Everyone wore frill or bow-trimmed, multicolored silks or satins, and she didn't stand out like a light post in the centre of a pond. Fortunately, she'd had time to modify the lacy gown she had worn to the Burleigh's ball.

Unfortunately, she was not sure that this resurrection had any more relationship to style than the original version, not now that she had seen the slim, graceful gowns worn by Essie Deering, and Mary Phillips, the other two young ladies who stepped into the carriage, whose chaperonage had been trusted to Nora.

The leading carriage contained the Gerard party, Lady Gerard taking charge of her own daughter and two others. After being dropped off, the two parties joined forces and entered the assembly room, travelling through the vestibule, the hair of everyone ahead of Cassia jauntily bouncing with each enthusiastic step. From an area at the back of the hall, the orchestra had a commanding view of the room. The older ladies found suitable seating along a row at the side. What with the tuning up of the musical instruments and the arrival of acquaintances, Cassia could barely hear herself think. The younger ladies pointed out people they knew while Lady Gerard nodded to others. Cassie recognized not a single person in the chattering crowd. She squared her shoulders, the words *a stranger in a strange land* repeating over and over in her head.

"Miss Lacey?"

Turning, she used her automatic smile, which died when she saw the devastatingly attractive, dark-haired duke. "Sir." She curtsied, her pulse fluttering in her throat. No woman in her right mind could fail to be overwhelmed by his appearance. Her heartbeat tripped and stumbled into a pathetic rhythm. Determined not to let him know his effect on her, she edged a little sideways and kept her posture rigidly under control.

"Please address me as Adam." He bowed. "With so many mutual friends, we should be on a first name basis. We shall be meeting everywhere and the formality of titles is not needed in such small groups."

"I'm honored, sir," she said in a cool voice, knowing that if she used the first name of a duke she would appear to be a bumptious social climber. "But I would find that rather awkward."

He drew a long, deep breath. "George asked me to watch over you tonight."

"He can watch over me himself." She turned her head away, embarrassed by his scrutiny of her face. Her cheeks warmed a little.

"He has another engagement. He wants to make sure you enjoy yourself. Little does he know he has deputized the fox to watch over the chicken."

Her spine relaxed. At least he knew she knew about his reputation. Yet again, she had raised her defences needlessly. The man couldn't hurt her because he would never fool her. He didn't have enough interest in her to try. "I'm hardly a chicken. More like a hen."

"Pecking at me every time I open my mouth."

"Surely not every time. How do you plan to watch over me?" She raised her eyebrows, as usual caught by his candid phrasing.

"I'll stay a foot away and frown at all your prospective dance partners." He pushed his hands deep into the pockets of his black knee breeches, staring at down at her, a calculating expression in his startling blue eyes.

"I don't doubt you would if you did. But would that amuse you?"

"More than you might think, though I suspect George didn't have that in mind. He wanted me to find suitable partners for you, and I shall do that."

"Suitable in what way?"

"Young and eligible, of course."

"Oh, dear. You'll be wasting the time of any eligible gentlemen. I'm not exactly available."

He stared at her for a moment, causing her skin to

prickle all over. His face had relaxed into an expression somewhat like amusement. Although she didn't stare, she noted his thick eyelashes. No man had the right to be so endowed. Although handsome in a stark male way, this feature softened his high-bridged nose and his determined mouth. Her face warmed and she glanced away.

He continued. "Regardless, when I am asked to perform a job, I do my utmost to succeed."

"If you succeed at finding interesting dancing partners, that is good enough for me. Introduce the eligible gentlemen to the other young ladies here who are seriously pursuing marriage."

He shrugged. "They can enjoy your cast offs."

She smiled with disbelieving amusement. "I'll expect a queue formed to the right."

"If you will do me the honor first, I'll be better able to show you off. That should advertise your presence nicely. You look rather interesting yourself tonight, I have to say."

The back-handed compliment caused a tightness in her spine. Even she knew that the white lace outfit she had worn to the Burleigh's ball last week had been frumpy. While Nora had been busy this morning, Cassia, no seamstress, had removed the organza sleeves, and removed the train. She now wore the lacy gown over her blue silk under-dress.

Copying the style she had worn last time, she had knotted her abundant hair at the crown of her head. Nora dithered a little when she saw this, being a great admirer of curls. However, whenever Cassia tried fancier hairstyles, she resembled a horse decorated with a garland. "Thank you," she said to the duke with a smile that she wished could have been more sincere. "Last time you decided I had worn my gown to match my name."

Hooding his gaze, he glanced down at her. "Clearly, I was trying to impress you with my tact."

"Unfortunately, you impressed me with your truthfulness instead."

"I am glad to hear I impressed you."

"With your truthfulness, sir. Not with your charm." She half turned away, not about to be trapped again into flirting with this careless male.

However, he touched her elbow, forcing her to glance at his perfectly sculptured face.

"Yes?"

"The music, Miss Lacey. My request to dance with you. Your lack of an answer. All of these statements come together awaiting your next word."

She grabbed a long breath. "Yes, your grace. I would just as soon be dancing as sitting and watching."

With that, he offered an elbow for her to attach a hand. He led her onto the floor, joining into a simple dance that gave her a chance to curtsey to a never-ending line of young gentlemen she had never met before. After the duke escorted her back to Nora, she wondered if she would see another partner, but apparently her blue and white outfit as shown by partnering a duke on the dance floor had impressed an adequate amount of young men to keep her occupied for the next four brackets. By this time, she had offered enough bland smiles to all and sundry to last her for the next week.

Finally, she placed herself firmly beside Nora on the

bank of seats. A swoosh of skirts beside her, and she glanced up.

"Are you sitting this one out, Cassia?" Cornelia Gerard wore a gauzy puce gown with darker ribbons around her waist. A petite young lady with mid brown hair, she looked lovely in the color.

"I certainly hope so. I'm quite exhausted. I haven't had so much exercise since I had to chase my horse around the paddocks at home." Cassia arranged her skirts neatly and adopted a forbidding expression to aim at a young approaching male. He veered and stood in front of Cornelia, who graciously accepted his hand for the next dance. Nora and Lady Gerard didn't break their enthusiastic discussion about pickling vegetables. If either lady had taken a breath, Cassia could have added her opinion of pickled cucumbers as well.

She eked out a sigh, idly watching the dancers swing by, while she tried spreading her cramped toes. The red velvet shoes that she had thought comfortable at home had decided to pinch. All that dancing had taken quite a toll on her feet, not that she hadn't enjoyed the exercise. The chair beside her creaked and she turned to see the duke settle himself beside her.

"I thought country girls had more stamina than city girls." His jacket sleeve pressed against her shoulder. "I'm surprised to see you taking a rest so early in the evening."

"We country girls' have positively dull lives compared to our city cousins who race around all day having gowns fitted, choosing hats, and trying to find suitable ribbons for trimmings."

He held her gaze, his hard mouth relaxing. "In that case,

I shall remove you from all this excitement. The supper room should be calming. The so-called supper won't be served for another hour."

"So called?"

"Stale bread and plain cake."

She smiled cautiously, rather enjoying his bluntness. "I must admit that I would like a little peace. I'm not used to so much chatter." In the midst of her gaze meeting his, her pulse began to throb. Somehow, the way his eyes met hers caused the muscles in her neck to tense.

His mouth curved with a half smile. Rising to his feet, he held out his arm to her. She moved her fingers cautiously toward his sleeve and he lifted his elbow so that her hand rested in the crook again. After a lingering glance at her stepmother, who still enthusiastically discussed salt measurements, she let herself be led into the supper room, where a few silent servants glided about filling the tables with sandwiches and sliced cake.

She focused back on the confident male who accompanied her, not quite sure she should be alone with him. "Do people often sit in here while the staff are working, sir?"

"I'm sure we wouldn't be the first to do so. Even if you won't call me Adam," he said, his gaze wandering over her face, "I have decided to call you Cassia." He led her to an alcove that boasted a view onto King Street. For a moment he stared into the darkness outside. "It's amazing how busy London has grown since I was a boy. I noticed the same thing when I came down from college."

She leaned back against the framing pillar, watching his face relax, which helped to ease her mind. "What did you study?"

He shrugged. "The classics. My father thought that anything else would be useless to a man who had everything. He was right. My younger brother studied law. That would be handy if he were interested in assisting me."

"He's not?"

"He is attempting to sew his wild oats first."

She almost smiled. "And yours are ready to harvest?" she asked eyeing him sideways.

He tilted his eyebrows, which added interest to his expression. "I'm not certain *what* you are asking but I am *certain* you shouldn't be asking. A man's dalliances are not discussed with the fairer sex."

"I suppose not, but the fairer sex hears about them, regardless." She forced out a mock exasperated breath.

"That's a weight off my mind. Do you wish to sit?" He indicated the group of chairs arranged around the table no more that three steps away.

"I think not. The staff would find that strange, as if we were waiting for service."

Although he moved closer to her, she stayed put, thinking she shouldn't let his size impress her and cause her to step back. Although she attempted to keep her poise, her cheeks began to warm. He radiated intensity. She wouldn't be female if she weren't fully aware this man occupied far more of her thoughts tonight than she had needed. With his eyes focused entirely on her, never had she been more conscious of forcing air in and out of her lungs. Her heart set up an inconsistent rhythm that rushed to the pulse in her neck.

His gaze intensified. He took her hand between his. Caught like a rabbit in a trap, she pondered pushing him away, she pondered stepping aside, and did neither. How gauche she would appear if she treated him like a suitor. She needed to let him know she wouldn't accept casual flirting.

Unfortunately, not a single sensible word came to her mind ... and then he straightened his fingers and pressed her gloved palm against his. His fingers meshed between hers. The strain of breathing and remaining rigid began to heat her skin. Although she knew she should take her hand back, and smile casually, she remained staring into his eyes.

Then her gaze focused on his sensuous mouth. Although he usually appeared somewhat harsh, he no longer looked quite so intense. His lips kicked up at the sides and his heavy eyelids half covered his eyes. Perhaps, because she saw him as a relaxed man rather than a person who was determined to do as he chose, she waited to see what his next move would be.

She cleared her throat, or she thought she did. Instead she swallowed, testing him or herself. Clearly he had brought her here to be alone with her, but had he planned all along to test her morals? Or was she a challenge to be won? As her heartbeat thundered loud enough to echo in her ears, she noted a faint scattering of silver flecked the stark blue of his irises. His beautiful, thick eyelashes ended with roots slightly paler than the tips.

He exhaled, his breath tickling her ear. While he kept his gaze on hers, he slowly loosened his grip on her hand. Wrapping one arm around her shoulder, he spanned his gloved fingers on the back of her neck as he moved her into his embrace. He smelled of starch and some sort of cologne, a rather nice combination. Sure by now that he intended to kiss her, she lifted her face while his other hand slid to the flat of her back. His mouth gently pressed on the curl of her upper ear.

Her breath came in spurts like silent gasps, but she didn't move, except to splay her hands on either side of his chest. Beneath the wool of his jacket, his body was as hard and inflexible as a brick wall. Although he was large enough to overpower her, she knew by his careful movements that he had no intention of doing so. Like her, he was waiting to see what would happen next. Although she didn't doubt that he would let her go if she asked, she remained silent. She wanted this man to make the decision about whether or not to kiss her. Only then could she decide whether to either push him away, or let him.

His face lost all expression. He arched her into him using his forearm. Dratted man. If he planned to kiss her, she wished he would begin, but he eased his grip, leaning back to examine her expression. Swallowing, she noted the wary narrowing of his eyes. He had nothing to be wary about. She couldn't harm a man his size, not that she wanted to. Instead she wanted her first kiss from him. He had teased her enough, and if he let her go now, she would know herself to have offered and been resisted.

Her hand gripped his lapel. His beautiful lashes flickered across her brow. His breath teased across her mouth. As each second ticked away, she wanted more and more to experience her first kiss with a man who clearly knew what he was doing.

Her whole body began to thud with uncontrollable need. When his lips finally touched hers, she slid both her hands beneath his jacket collar, lifted her face and finally her mouth pressed against his. She expected herself to move away, her task achieved, but his delicate touch, soft and sparing, imbued a need in her. His chest expanded, he stiffened, and lifted his lips. He met her stunned gaze, and dipped his head again, tasting her mouth, hesitating, and starting all over again, while she held tightly to his lapels.

Perhaps she stopped breathing. Apparently, he had no qualms about continuing the kiss, but still his lips teased her rather than sating her need.

Then his hold dropped to her waist and he lifted her lower body closer. She stiffened. Although she knew about his experience, she hadn't expected him to treat her like a loose woman.

"I think it's time we stopped," he murmured into her ear.

Even before he had finished speaking, she came to her senses. Her cheeks hot with embarrassment, she wriggled out of his grip. How she came to have behaved with such a lack of decorum she could only blame on his expertise in leading women astray. Heaving in a breath, she stepped back.

His eyebrows lifted. "I warned you."

"I wasn't quite sure you were as disreputable as I had heard."

He considered the expression on her face. "And your conclusion is ... "

She gathered up the shreds of her dignity by remembering her posture. "Guilty as charged." Unfortunately, her voice sounded husky and she needed to swallow.

His lips twitched, and he half nodded as if acknowledging a hit. If he laughed she would stamp on his foot.

"I think it's time I joined the others," she said turning

with such force that the swing of her shawl left the fringe caught on the buttons of his jacket.

"You will need to wait until I have removed the ties that bind us." He glanced down and took his time untangling the fringe. When he had freed himself, he squared his magnificent shoulders.

All along, she had been right about him. He had been trying to see how far a duke could take an unsophisticated countrywoman. Even if he didn't kiss and tell, he would see her as a woman of easy virtue like those with whom he mainly associated. Her lesson in humiliation was now complete and she would now stay away from him forever.

He stood staring at her with a blank expression on his face. "I am expecting you to apologize for using me."

"Using you? You weren't the one backed up against a pillar."

His autocratic eyebrows lifted. "I was the one grasped by the lapels."

She gasped. "I was caught between a pillar and you."

For a moment he stood completely still. "You only had to say one single word."

"You could have used the same word," she said coldly. "I hope you will behave responsibly from now on."

"I'm known for my responsible behavior."

Infuriated, she gritted her teeth. "You are the most despicable man I have ever met."

"At this stage, I think you will have to accept that we no longer strangers."

The embarrassment that she had refused to admit colored her cheeks. "I'm certain you don't imagine that I want your friendship."

His gaze focused over her shoulder, and then back at her. He lowered his voice to an undertone. "Your sweet little step-mama has just arrived. Please try to act as if you haven't been enticing hapless men into corners."

"Says the spider to the fly," she said in a sheeted whisper between her teeth. She swung around, making sure she stepped in front of the disgraceful duke. "Nora. Have you been looking for me?"

"I don't mean to interrupt but Lady Gerard asked about you and I couldn't see you anywhere." Nora's gaze wavered between Cassia and Huntsdale.

"I came in here to reinvigorate myself and I certainly did that. Now I'm ready to dance the night away."

Nora glanced at Huntsdale, but didn't say a word. Cassia took her arm and hustled her back to the entrance. "The duke was kind enough to accompany me," she said in a cool voice, realizing he stood right behind her. "Thank you, sir."

"I'm glad I helped you to invigorate yourself," he said as he opened the door for her to pass through.

She didn't deign to meet his gaze.

Her next partner was a polite young man who was somehow related to Lady Gerard. He treated her as a gentleman should treat a lady, with a smile, and keeping his distance. He wouldn't push a lady up against a pillar and kiss her until she couldn't catch her breath. He wouldn't mock her with his every word.

Then she danced with Huntsdale's brother, Jeremy Everley, who was great fun, lighthearted and amusing. Cornelia Gerard eyed her when Mr. Everley brought her back to the party and she managed to edge closer to him, but he didn't ask her to dance. He wandered over to another party and chose a young lady with thick curls hanging in a bunch at the back of her head, and a high-pitched laugh.

"His mother would turn in her grave," Cornelia muttered. "He has the worst taste in women of anyone I know."

"Have you known him for a long time?" Cassia asked, noticing a rip in her hem.

"He lived with us when his brother was up at Oxford. He is practically family, though."

"You don't know the duke quite as well?"

"He has always been a friend of my brother, Bertie. They attended Eton together before Oxford. He was Lord Chiltern then. But they're older, of course."

Cassia nodded. The distance between nineteen and twenty-eight was quite a gulf, especially when the nineteen year-old was as fresh as a daisy and the twenty-eight year old was a dangerous womanizer. And here she sat, a twenty-five year old countrywoman, not quite fresh, but not quite sophisticated either. "He has a reputation with the ladies."

"Who? The duke? He never comes to the balls. He takes his duties seriously, you know. Jeremy is the one with the reputation. He flirts with everyone." Cornelia sounded put out.

"He's the right age to flirt. And the duke is the right age to take his duties seriously." And Cassia hoped he would be doing so instead of attending the next ball. She wasn't sure why she had been singled out by him and she had the dreadful idea that she may have been his idea of an *easy* woman. She had wanted him to kiss her, and she hardly knew him. She certainly knew his reputation but somehow she had let herself be drawn to him for the second time. But of course, an experienced male would know exactly how to do that to a woman.

However, the duke had no scruples and she couldn't allow him to overrun hers. She would take care to keep out of his way the next time she saw him.

Chapter Four

Adam rued kissing Cassia. Although he had seen a clear invitation on her face, his tactics had been poor. If he had remained staring at her mouth, she would have made the first move, and not put him on the wrong foot. He also should not have told her she enjoyed the experience. She wasn't the type of woman to be told she had thoughts and desires. His methodology had been poor, and he had learned that she didn't see him as human, after all. All she could see was a duke who should be taught a lesson by a woman who had no intention of letting her needs guide her.

Consequently, he revised his strategy, determined to regain his hard won foothold with her. Tonight, he would attend Gerard's ball, his third ball in a row, a number he had not imagined reaching in any year. After choosing the ballroom knot for his cravat, a high, simple crossover, he then rethought his waistcoat, finally asking his valet for the plain black to meld with his black jacket and knee breeches.

Placing his gold fob into his pocket, he strode downstairs to the drawing room and stopped in the doorway. Lord Lucien Walton sat in Adam's favorite leather armchair, sipping sherry. "I thought I was meant to pick you up."

Redheaded Lucien nodded, taking another sip. "I told your butler to leave me here with a bottle. I met Jeremy at White's and he brought me back with him. Saves time, since we all plan to go to the same place." A man with a jaw as stubborn as his nature, Lucien had inherited a small estate from his maternal uncle. He lived in an elegant set of rooms and ate out most of the time, which saved money on hiring a decent cook, or so he said. "He's gone upstairs to change."

Adam moved over to the couch, keeping his expression casual. "Do you remember Miss Cassia Lacey?"

"Of course. I saw her two days ago and danced with her at the assembly rooms last week."

"If you see me with her tonight, don't butt in. Leave me some privacy."

"If I recall," Lucien said, checking his cuff links, "I left you with her at Almack's. I'm not too sure she came back into the ballroom entirely pleased with you."

"I'm not sure, either. I'm hoping to redeem myself." Adam impatiently tapped the arm of the chair.

Lucien scrutinized his face. "That's not like you, old chap. I didn't think you cared a toss about anyone's opinion."

"In the main, I don't, but the woman interests me." Adam evaded Lucien's gaze.

The other man shook his head. "Seems to me that you

have had your nose put out of joint. and you see that as a challenge."

"Could be, but I could also be thinking about marriage. It's time. Who better than a woman who doesn't cater to my every wish?"

"I understand how boring that would be for you." Lucien smiled sardonically. "As for me, I would be forever grateful if I could find a woman who catered to mine."

Adam shrugged. "I have servants who do so. My wife, when I marry, will be someone who can run my home without constantly asking for my input." He rubbed the back of his neck. "It's for Jeremy as well as for me. He's running wild. If we had a calming influence in the house, if I could look around the house and see polished wood, flowers, cheerful servants who didn't wander about moving everything until I have to ask where I ..." He could only express his rational reasons for wanting Cassia. Frivolous reasons like finding pleasure in her voice, seeing the humor in her eyes, or noting that his breath shortened and his cock hardened when his gaze caught hers had to remain his, and his alone, despite those being his foremost needs.

"It sounds to me as if you want a good housekeeper." Lucien grinned, companionably. "You should ask George if he could recommend someone."

"I want one who can entertain a houseful of guests and charm my friends. George's housekeeper charms George. Cassia isn't frivolous and she is experienced in running a household. I heard that from her father. Also, she's easy on the eye. None of those other little ninnies has any conversation. None would correct me."

"So you want a housekeeper who corrects you?"

Adam lifted his shoulders. He wanted Cassia in his bed but he wouldn't tell Lucien that Cassia had him completely rattled. Only a week ago, she had kissed him as if she wanted to progress farther and then she had informed him that he didn't interest her in the least. Her response had certainly indicated otherwise. His had been inconvenient at the time. "One who can stand on her own two feet and doesn't need constant attention from me."

Lucien swirled his sherry around in his glass. "I have no objection to you trying your luck. Do you mind if I ask her to dance?"

"Make sure you don't get any ideas."

Lucien tapped the pads of his fingers together. "What about George? I thought she was his special friend."

"He won't be there tonight. He was called back home on Tuesday. I don't know when he'll be back."

"I meant what about George's plans for her."

"He has none. He gave me free rein."

"Everyone ready?" Jeremy bounced into the room like the pup he was. "Heigh ho. It should be fun tonight. Lady Gerard is letting her younger daughters stay up for the first dance. I'm promised to Daisy for that one. She said she has been practicing her steps for weeks."

Adam rose and bumped his fist onto the side of Jeremy's shoulder. "She's a trifle too young for you, isn't she?"

"Ha ha." Jeremy stretched his lips into a sarcastic grin. "Fifteen, I think. It won't be long before she is making her debut. I never thought Cornelia would either but now she is. I can't imagine *her* a married lady. She is such a prissy little miss."

"Do you have any intentions there?" Adam queried his

brother with his eyes. Jeremy and Cornelia had known each other since birth, like Cassia and George. Jeremy was almost a fixture in the Gerard household. Adam used to be, after the death of his parents, but once he had accepted his responsibilities, his spare time was minimal and mainly spent at his club or gambling with his cronies. He no longer needed the Gerard's generous guidance.

"Like marrying Cornelia? Lord no. I don't want to be shackled any time soon—too many pretty girls to sample first."

Lucien rose to his feet and placed his empty glass on the mantelpiece, which happened to be one of the few available surfaces. The rest of the room was filled with clutter, like books, empty vases, statuettes, a dried flower arrangement, which Adam must ask to have removed, packs of cards, a chess set, and, amazingly, a miniature set of farm animals. He picked up one, wondering who and why this had been left here. The servants removed food and wine, but never his or Jeremy's property. "Your brother appears to have another idea entirely."

"What?" Jeremy led the way out of the room. "He doesn't want to sample pretty girls? I thought that was why he gave up Mrs. Smith."

"You gave up Mrs. Smith?" Lucien lifted his eyebrows.

Adam shrugged. "The time had come for us to part. And Lucien, not another word about the subject we were discussing."

Lucien touched his forehead as if acknowledging a direct order from a senior officer. He also grinned. Adam knew he could trust his friend. Lucien had a propensity to play practical jokes but he had always been loyal.

Adam's carriage took the group to Upper Belgrave Street where the Gerard family resided. Carriages filled the street, harnesses jingling, and the drivers hailed one another in shouts. Amid the chaos, Adam and his companions clambered out of the conveyance, the driver having been asked to return at midnight. Although heavy gray clouds skulked in the sky, Adam assumed the impending rain would hold off until then, preferring not to dice with his coachman's health.

An arched canopy covered the path to the Gerard's open front door. Light blared out into the street. Once inside the doorway, Adam bowed to Sir Patrick and Lady Gerard, who stood in the spacious hall, greeting guests.

"How smart you gentlemen look." Lady Gerard was kissed on the cheek by Jeremy, and then Adam and Lucien. "Take yourselves into the ballroom and do whatever young gentlemen do."

"Which gives one the impression that she doesn't know what young gentlemen really do," Jeremy said in an undertone as he led the way to the green painted ballroom, which comprised the dining and sitting rooms with their connecting doors folded back. "Bertie should have given her a few pointers." The orchestra had set up in the corner since the house hadn't been built with a minstrel's gallery.

Adam shook his head. "I'm sure she does but her kind heart wouldn't allow her to tell us to go inside and drink too much to cover our conversational inadequacies and our missteps on the dance floor."

"Speak for yourself. I've been waltzing since I was a lad. Her daughters have had me as a practice dance partner forever. Yo. Cornelia." Jeremy smiled across the room as pretty little Cornelia Gerard waved him over to join a group of other pretty young ladies. "Come on, fellows. Duty calls, though one of that lot wouldn't in any man's wildest dreams be seen as a duty."

Adam agreed. Cassia stood tall and elegant in blue. She again wore the severe hairdo that emphasized the beauty of her facial structure. And the moment she caught his gaze, she turned her back on him. Tonight would be long. His shoulders slipped a little but he didn't deviate because he had noticed Jeremy's target, a dark haired beauty with enormous eyes. When he reached the group, he did his duty and asked Cornelia for the pleasure of the first waltz. The look on her face said she would rather Jeremy had asked her but Jeremy stood transfixed in front of the beauty.

Adam took the beauty to the floor for the second dance. Meanwhile, dancing partners lined up for Cassia. He thought about leaving but he couldn't let her have that victory. Until supper was served, he stayed out of her way while keeping her in his sights, which ended up being a good tactic because although she left for the supper table, she omitted an escort. Every time she reached for a morsel to fill her plate, someone stepped in front of her. Adam moved closer and filled a plate. "Take this," he said to her, keeping his expression cool.

"I would prefer to choose the food I want, thank you." She lifted her determined chin.

He sucked in a breath. "Then if you would like to point, I will fill your plate with whatever you want. And by the way, I would like to apologize for my behavior the last time we met."

"It's of no significance."

"You're in no danger from me," he said in an undertone.

"... says the fox to the chicken."

He almost smiled. "I admit I made a mistake."

"Swayed as you were by my beauty."

He shrugged. "By your laugh. By your attitude. Tonight I could be swayed by your beauty were I not on my best behavior."

"You're incorrigible."

He caught her gaze. "Perhaps."

She stared at him, her eyes narrowed. "Yes, you may fill my plate if you promise to go away."

"An intriguing choice but ..." He inclined his head in assent. "I'll fill your plate." And he did so. Then he left, glad to see that she didn't look as pleased to see the back of him as she might have.

For the next hour, he danced with the ladies who had debuted some years earlier and who didn't tell him to go away. His ego assuaged, he checked his fob watch. Only half an hour to go until midnight. He hoped Cassia's evening's entertainment had been as ordinary as his, and that by the next time they met she would be more amenable to his pursuit of her. He couldn't interest her by showing his interest in her and he couldn't interest her by faking disinterest. A man who only knew how to manage a frontal attack had little hope with a testing woman like her.

As he pondered trying again, he saw her back to the French doors that faced the garden. She opened one a crack, and took a step backward. In the snap of a finger, she disappeared. He hesitated for less than half a minute before he followed. As he stepped into the garden, eddies of wind whipped at his coattails.

The air hovered thick with moisture. A light veil of rain misted across his face. Cassia appeared to be heading for the mews. He couldn't imagine why anyone would sneak out of a ballroom during the beginning of a rainstorm—unless she had an assignation. His chest tightened with an emotion somewhat akin to bloody-mindedness.

Raindrops began to splat. Then a sheet pelted down, sweeping across the landscape. Cassia gathered up her skirts and ran to the lane at the back. He followed, racing toward the shelter of the carriage house. Cassia spotted him as he neared her. She veered into the feed shed. He knew by her mulish expression that she contemplated shutting the door in his face but fortunately she saved him the effort of pushing his way in. "We meet again." He tried to sound astonished.

"You were following me." Her mouth set into a firm line.

"You seemed to know where you were going." Water dripped from his hair to his shoulders. He flicked his head and the spray shot around him. Becoming acclimatized to the dark, he noted that she looked a trifle damp but she had reached the outbuilding a few seconds before the heaviest downpour and the damage to her gown was minimal. He brushed the collection of raindrops from the shoulders of his jacket.

She moved back, apparently caught by a drop or two. "You really are a pest."

"You may be grateful for my jacket if you are planning to return to the ballroom."

"Of course I'm planning to return." She folded her arms.

"Who are you meeting? I'm fairly sure he'll wait for the downpour to end before you see him out here."

"You think I might meet a man in the stables? Why? Who wouldn't I be able to speak to in the ballroom?"

"There's that. Then, why on earth did you come out here?"

"Homesickness," she said in a fraught voice. "I wanted to be somewhere real. Ballrooms aren't a part of my life."

"So, you're more at home in the feed shed. I wouldn't have guessed that."

She gave an impatient sigh. "Until I opened the door, I didn't know this was a feed shed. I saw it as a shelter. My plan was to walk in the garden by myself for a while. I didn't expect the downpour."

"Clouds give the first warning."

"Therefore, I'm meeting someone." She lifted up her stubborn chin. "Best you go before he spots you."

"I'll wait with you. I don't know how we got off on the wrong foot and I don't know why you're so set against me."

"You are a dangerous man. You are well-enough looking to turn the head of an impressionable young woman. But you are so very disreputable."

He stepped back, surprised. "Disreputable? I doubt that is my reputation."

"It would be with any woman you have kissed. It certainly is with those who know that you have a private association that no decent woman would mention."

For a moment he wondered who had told her about Mellie. "Are you hinting you are not decent?"

"Please don't think you need to keep me company."

He stiffened his jaw, staring at her outline, which appeared to be rigid. A horse nickered somewhere behind him. A wall separated the shed from the stables. The unromantic smell of wet straw and horse manure hung in the air. Despite this last, his attraction toward her was undiminished. He wanted to grab her into his arms and rest his face on her hair, and hold her until she relaxed against him. He wanted her to see him as he really was, a hungry man, and not a privileged duke who used to have a mistress.

"As soon as the rain stops, I would like you to leave," she said in a bored voice. "I won't be returning with you in case someone spots us and assumes we had an assignation."

He mulled her order, wishing he knew how to explain himself, but his pride would not allow him to grovel. Telling her he had given up his mistress because he wanted a woman he hardly knew would brand him as a fool. So, he watched the downpour lashing at the trees while she picked around the shed. The rain thundered on the slate roof and the wind blew up a gale. Eddies passed through the boards on the walls and swirled around his ankles.

"How disappointing," she said, close behind him. Her breath whispered across the back of his neck. "This place is not as large as it seems from the outside."

"It's a storage shed but it's connected to the stables. Other than me, you might find a cat or two in here, or even a few mice."

"I found the straw bales instead," she said in a voice that refused to contemplate mice.

"Let me make a seat for you while we wait for the storm to pass over."

She gave a loud sigh but appeared to acquiesce. "That would be very kind," she drawled, her voice so patronizing that he needed to rethink his tactics. As an oldest son and the possessor of a fortune, he was used to being heard and taking charge. He had no doubt that she knew she was testing his limit.

By the light of the moon, he lifted down two of the top bails and placed them in front of the stack, in view of the open door. Then he stood back, making an extravagant flourishing gesture. "Your throne, my lady," he said in his formal ducal voice.

She eyed him as she sat precisely, her hands clasped in her lap. Her curvy shape in the nightshades of gray gave her a softer appearance. Not that he needed her to be soft with him. He enjoyed the push and pull of her, the way she lured him on with her intelligence and then drew him into a sudden stop when she lost control of the conversation.

"Are you in love with your mistress?" Her voice held a tone of mollification mixed with curiosity.

He shrugged. "I no longer have a mistress. I wasn't in love with her but in a way I loved her." He sat beside her, not too close, the intimacy of the dark cloaking him with invulnerability. Right now, he could be anyone talking to her, not a rejected suitor or even a man. "If I hadn't had feelings for her, our association would have been unlikely. But the time came that I decided she shouldn't be in her position and we parted ways."

"What made you come to that decision?" Her fingers clutched at each other.

He didn't intend to flatter this woman who would have none him by telling her the truth, that he wanted her, and only her. "Perhaps I needed to put my house in order rather than use hers." He stared straight ahead while the wind crashed the door against the outside of the shed.

She gave a low soft laugh. "I can't pretend to understand the words you just said, other than you were avoiding something by being with her."

"I suspect I was, but—" The door shivered in the wind, and while he watched in amazement, the heavy wood swung, teetered, and then with a huge renewed effort slammed against the frame. The bar clattered into place. Suddenly the area turned as black as pitch. Once before, he had been in this room when the door had closed unexpectedly, but he had been with Jeremy. For a moment he sat, undecided. "Now we have no moon to watch over us."

"It's nicer with the door open. I'm not afraid of mice or cats but I don't particularly like being in the dark."

He slowly arose. "In that case, I'll open the door again." Slits of pale light showed through the join of the door to the frame. He ran his hand over the top of the doorframe and but he didn't find the implement he could use to lift the latch. He pushed at the heavy wood. "Perhaps it's working with the wind. Come over and help me rattle the thing."

Cassia arrived as a perfumed presence, and rattled the frame with him. The door didn't budge with the two of them shoving every which way. "I didn't notice," she said. "Did the door have a lock or a bar?"

"A bar."

She remained silent. "There might be a tool in here we could use to lift it."

"Did you notice anything while you were wandering around?"

"The bales are tied with twine. I didn't see any tools. Perhaps a good hearty shove will break the lock."

He grabbed the door and shook, rattling the hinges again but making not a jot of difference.

She stood behind him. "Perhaps something in here will break down the door."

"That seems a little harsh on our hosts."

"We're locked in here in the middle of the night. I'm sure they will forgive us."

"I'll see if I can find anything else." He moved backward, tripping over the seating bale in the process. For a few minutes, he grappled around, but he knew he would find nothing.

His coach would have arrived at the front of the house by now. His brother or Lucien would search for him. Where they might imagine he had gone, he couldn't tell, but he doubted they would lose a night's sleep over his disappearance. In the past, he had left functions before the end, either taking a convenient hackney or if he used his own coach, sending his driver back for the others later. As long as his transport arrived for the others, matters would proceed normally. Certainly no one would check where he had gone.

After wasting a reasonable amount of time, he felt his way back to the straw bale. "I'm very much afraid that we are imprisoned here for the time being." His voice filled the darkness and seemed to echo back at him.

"For the time being, what?" she asked, her wary voice coming from the far side of the shed.

"Until someone either misses us or arrives in the morning to feed the horses." He leaned back against the bales, the dark night hiding his expression. Out of all the places in the world to seduce a woman, one of the last he would choose would be a feed shed. However, he had wanted to be left alone with her so that he had a chance to put his case.

He had to take his chance now, or he would possibly never have another.

Chapter Five

Cassia paced, swishing her skirts nervously as the straw shuffled beneath her feet. She had hoped for the sound of voices. Her heart beat a pitter-pat as she rested the side of her face on the rough wooden door, but she could hear nothing other than shingles rattling on the roof and the wind soughing through the rafters. Peering through the chink, she saw the bar that held the door closed. Then the moon hid behind dark clouds.

Her breathing fluttered like a bird flying into a storm. Being shut in a dark enclosed space with a large intimidating stranger put terrifying thoughts in her mind. Using her outstretched hands to seek the way ahead, she took a step toward the hay bales. And another. A presence loomed up beside her. She reared back with an involuntary gasp.

"Give me your hand." Huntsdale's voice sounded hushed in the dark. He touched her waist.

The intimacy of his action stiffened her spine, but his hand on her appeared to be a guiding hold, moving her slightly to one side until her calves rested against a hay bale.

She groped behind and realized that she could sit. Not about to let him know that she appreciated his help, she flicked off his hold, and gingerly settled herself down. In the assembly rooms, with no more than a narrow-eyed glance from her, this man had ignored the boundaries of civilized behavior. Knowing his propensity to cross the line, she needed to make sure she said nothing that might sound even slightly friendly. Unable to see more than the angled chink of light around the door, she sat rigid. "I expect that when Nora is ready to go home, she will search for me," she said, in what she hoped sounded like a warning to him that she was not unsupported.

"Would she expect to find you in a hay barn?" Huntsdale sat beside her, close enough to brush her arm with his.

She shivered, though not with cold. The hay prickled against her back and she turned to see his face. "When she can't find me elsewhere she will have someone look outside. Shall you be missed?"

"Not until my carriage comes to collect me. That would be about now. We shouldn't be stuck in here too much longer."

"You sound confident." By narrowing her eyes, she could almost make out his features in the dark.

He didn't answer. The mist of rain captured in her hair from outside turned into a cold drizzle on the sides of her bare neck. She cupped each elbow with the opposite gloved hand and tried to imagine being warm. Her chin wobbled in a miserable shiver. She hated the dark and the ridiculous situation into which she had put herself.

He leaned sideways, shifting around. Suddenly the warmth of his jacket settled across her shoulders. She clutched at the sides, pulling the body-warmed fabric around her, wishing she had the pride to refuse his offer, but she thought she had never been so cold in her life. Fear contributed as much as the drizzly weather. Glad not to be able to summon up graciousness, she muttered, "Thank you."

"You're half naked while I wear many layers."

She gritted her teeth. "I am not half naked."

"Damn. That thought has been keeping me warm. Now I might need my jacket back."

"Take it, then." She stiffened, but not with outrage—with bloody-mindedness. Even in this difficult situation, he was ready to make a joke of her. "If you want to be a cad."

"I would prefer not to be a cad. Perhaps you can accept that I don't need the jacket and you do."

Even the forced patience in his tone humiliated her, but a woman who needed a jacket had to appear as if she deserved one. Wrapped in the second-hand warmth of his body, she sat, staring at the unwavering door, awaiting rescue from his coachman. "You must always have the last word, mustn't you?"

"I will admit that is one of my failings. And what are yours, my perfect icicle?"

She shifted around until she made herself as comfortable as she could, given the rigidity of the prickles beneath her, while she decided that she would rather respond than shiver nervously. "Too many to count."

"Start with the worst."

Her eyes narrowed. "My worst is my inability to take orders from dukes in feed-sheds."

"That's not your worst."

"Are you now about to tell me what my worst failing is? What about yours?" "Go ahead. What is my worst failing?"

"Your absolute certainty that you are always right."

He remained silent for a few seconds. "Should I be uncertain?"

"You could be a little less right," she said, frowning.

"So, I *am* always right?"

"You sound as though you think you are." Although she kept her tone haughty, conversation with this annoying man had begun to warm her. That, and his jacket.

"Why would I want to think I am wrong when I make statements?"

"See? You can't bear being told you are not always right." She didn't want to, but she almost smiled in the dark.

"When have I been wrong?"

"It's your attitude I am complaining about, not your ability to think."

He remained silent for a moment or two. "Perhaps I am slightly arrogant. But I'm a first son. I was given everything my heart desired until my brother was born. Then I was given everything first. I never had to think of myself as unimportant because I wasn't treated that way. You're an only child. I'm sure you also suffer from an amount of spoiling."

She nodded, although he couldn't see her. "Yes, the only difference being that I am not a boy. My father would have given everything he owned to have a son, and now he has one."

"Your stepmother is still young. I am sure she will want more than one."

"She now has three. She has two from her first marriage."

"Another is not unlikely."

Cassia made a dissatisfied mouth. "I know."

"I'm sure you will be a great help to her when she has the next."

His dry tone alerted her to the fact that he thought the opposite. She turned her head, narrowing her gaze to see him in the dark. "So, you assume I won't be?"

"I can't imagine you running around after another woman's children."

"You're right," she said with reluctance. "The baby is fortunately cared for by his nanny, but my step-brothers are constantly underfoot. The three of them already supplant me. Soon they'll be grown men and telling me what to do."

"I wouldn't dare tell you what to do."

"Then you have a greater sense of self preservation than I imagined."

"I think in most instances you know what to do without being told, unlike your pretty stepmother who appears to need instruction from you."

Cassia stared down at her lap. Nora didn't need instruction, not if she wanted to change the way the house was run. She only needed instruction in the way Cassia ran the house. "Should I not let her know what I think?"

"Is it wise to let her rely on you? You are a beautiful woman. You won't be left to languish on the shelf." He picked up and held her gloved hand between his two.

If his grip had been anything other than casual, she would have taken her hand back. Instead she resisted the temptation to warm the other between his, as well. "I can't see myself languishing anywhere. There is far too much I want to do."

"Yes. I feel that way myself. I'm trying to maintain my various interests as well as Jeremy's. I don't have enough hours in the day to run my household."

"Don't you have a housekeeper?"

"Of course. She runs the house and I have a secretary. He is meant to deal with the housekeeper but apparently I keep him too busy. He manages the servants well enough but not the way my mother did."

"No one ever does as well as the lady of the house." She wished she hadn't voiced her feelings quite so wistfully now that she wasn't the lady of the house.

"This season, I am expecting to find a lady for *my house*." He took her other hand too, and rubbed both together between his gloved hands.

A pulse in her throat thudded. Suddenly she seemed to have too much saliva in her mouth and she needed to swallow. "I wish you every success but I'm sure your wealth will do the job."

"I wasn't talking about paying a woman to run my house. I'm rather set on marriage."

"Oh? Your reputation says otherwise."

"Do you always listen to salacious gossip?"

Not quite sure what 'salacious' meant, she lowered her head, knowing that she blushed in the dark. "You have already admitted that you have a mistress."

"*Had*, not have. And if you are hinting that I ought to have married her …"

"No one would expect you to marry a fallen woman," she said, surprised.

"Even if I was the cause of her downfall? Shame on you, Cassia. Dislike me if you must, but don't dislike a member of your sex for being human."

Justly rebuked, she raised her chin. "A true gentleman wouldn't take a woman unless in marriage."

"I am merely an aristocrat. I can't lay claim to being a gentleman." He still sounded perfectly calm.

Brought to her senses, Cassia tried to take her hands back. She shouldn't be sitting in the dark holding hands with a self-confessed rogue. "See how you always try to prove you are not in the wrong?" She firmed her jaw. "The worst of it is, that in this case, you are. Not for using a woman outside of marriage, but about me. I am judgmental and it's another of my faults. I would like to be a better person."

He tightened his grip for a moment before he let her go. "By the by, if your hands are cold, any time you wish, I'll warm them again. I don't suffer the cold the way you do and I'm prepared to leave you with the only other one of my assets that I can offer you at this time."

She settled his jacket more closely around her, fully appreciating the first asset and his generosity in making sure she thought he didn't need his coat. Though, possibly he didn't. He, at least, had shirtsleeves and a waistcoat. She had nothing but a low-necked, cap-sleeved ball gown. The fabric of his coat emitted the faint tang of wet wool, neither unpleasant nor unfamiliar. "We're going to appear very foolish when we're found, you know," she said dolefully, realizing how much she had begun to enjoy the give and take of his conversation.

"We'll certainly have some explaining to do."

"You'll come off worse than I. I came outside for fresh air. You followed me."

He gave a soft considering hum. "My following you seems credible. I'm not certain you will sound so innocent. Young ladies don't leave balls alone. They go outside for assignations."

"Says the voice of experience."

For a moment, he said nothing, then, "Perhaps I ought to try the door again." The hay rustled and he shifted. His warmth left.

"No," he said from the doorway. "I can rattle the hinges but I can't shift the bar. I can't hear rain, though. If the downpour has stopped, someone is more likely to look outside for you. Do you commonly investigate the mews of your hosts?"

"No," she answered, her voice wavering, well aware of her breach of etiquette. "I usually don't do more than wander off in other people's gardens." She thought she should explain further in case he thought she was eccentric. "I like to see which plants thrive where, or how they look when they are fully grown. I'm designing a new one for my family home, you see. My mother started a plan the year before she died. Nora isn't interested."

"That's not surprising," he said, his breath shifting a tendril of her hair as he sat beside her again. "She would hardly want to work on a memorial to her husband's first wife."

She thought over his words. Realizing that she had been needlessly defensive, she relaxed a little, snuggling his jacket around her, and leaning her shoulders onto the hay bales behind to make herself more comfortable. Inappropriate or not, for discussing her family situation with a virtual stranger wouldn't change a thing, at least continuing this conversation would help take her mind off the unfortunate situation. Other than with George, she rarely spoke to men her age. With most people, she kept to safe subjects rather than gossipy tidbits from her real life, not at all keen to bore people, but the darkness seemed to need filling, even if only with small talk. "Do you think I should leave the garden for Nora to do with as she likes?" she asked carefully.

"Does she like gardening?"

"I don't know. I have been selfish about the garden because it's all I have left to do now that I don't run the house." More than likely, a duke couldn't sympathize with a woman who had a desperate need to be occupied. She blew out an impatient breath. "I have no useful role in life, and now this."

The brush of his arm indicated that he turned. "*This?* Being locked in the hay barn with me?"

"Not at all. I'm blaming her for my desperate rush to get married."

"It doesn't seem to be succeeding."

"And it won't. I decided whom I would marry when I was ten. My mind hasn't changed."

"Has his?"

"If so, he hasn't said a thing."

"If he hasn't said a thing, more than likely he doesn't know you intend to marry him."

"Of course he does." Although sure of George, she drew her eyebrows together while she considered the thought. "We've been promised to each other forever. His mother certainly thinks that I will be her daughter-in-law.

She discusses the household arrangements with me every time I visit."

"It's settled then. If his mother wants you, he doesn't stand a chance."

She fidgeted with her glove buttons. "You're speaking as if marriage to me would seem quite appalling to a man."

"You *are* rather set in your opinions. And you're a very managing sort of woman. At the picnic in Surrey, you had every table organized and woe betide anyone who didn't sit in the right place."

"The picnic at Surrey? Oh, yes. I do recall meeting you there, but I beg your pardon," she said in her haughtiest voice, crossing her arms beneath his jacket. "I did no such thing. Of course I had the tables organized. Who else would? But I didn't know who would be there. George gave me the numbers and that was all. I made three tables of eight. That meant that every person at each table could speak to everyone else. Anyone who wanted to move was welcome."

"As I recall, you asked people to move halfway through the meal."

"I asked *half* the people to move."

He gave a gruff sort of a laugh. "The men. And you say you didn't manage a thing?"

"Did anyone object? No. That's because no one was stuck with anyone they didn't want to be with for more than half the time."

"But those who might have wanted to be stuck became unstuck because of you."

"Personally," she said smoothly, "I was very glad to have lost at least one of the men beside me halfway through."

"I didn't feel the same way. I liked the woman on my left. Young Essie. She is a very pleasant companion."

"I don't think you said more than four words to her." Cassia clamped her lips together. Although she had tried to pretend she didn't recall meeting him, she knew very well that she had been on Huntsdale's right, and that she had been so taken with him that she had monopolized him. Now, she realized that the best thing that had happened to her was moving him to the other table and replacing his space, because George had warned her about Huntsdale's mistress before Cassia had time to make a complete fool of herself. She had thought Huntsdale was the most interesting man she had ever met. His blue eyes had fixed with hers until her breath shortened and her mouth stretched into a silly smile. She had flirted and she wasn't dainty enough to be a flirty woman.

"I let her talk. Women like talking more than men. We are better at nodding and agreeing."

"You really are impossible," she said as more of a sighing statement than a real criticism. By now she knew she couldn't flatten him with her words. Somehow the untenable situation in which they had found themselves had grown into an interesting sparring match.

"I don't have to be, Cassia. I could also be very possible."

She turned her head away from him. "I'm sure you could."

"Why don't you give me a chance?"

"Because I don't care to be trifled with," she said reluctantly.

"I'm not trifling. I'm not in the habit of kissing respectable women."

She tried to see his expression in the dark, but although she could make out his face, the depth of his gaze caused her to cease her close scrutiny. "Do I take it that you see me as less than respectable?"

"You take it that I acted unusually. You might ask yourself why."

"I can only speculate. Perhaps you made a bet that you could; perhaps you wanted to know if I was as respectable as I think I am."

"Nothing of the sort." His voice sighed out. "From the moment I met you, I liked you. I like the way you smile. Your mouth lifts at the edges, and you almost have a dimple in each cheek. Not quite, but you have a friendly crease there. I like the way you laugh as if you have been surprised into doing so. I like that you can talk to me without flirting. I like that you are a managing sort of woman." He picked up her closest hand and meshed his fingers with hers in a companionable way.

"You shouldn't worry. My glove is keeping my hand warm," she said, her tone embarrassingly husky.

"If your hands are cold, skin to skin contact works best. I can warm you better if I remove my gloves. Will you allow me?"

She imagined he could see her reluctant nod because he peeled off his first glove and then the second. When he picked up her hand again, she understood what he meant, for his toasty hot skin warmed right through her glove.

"And if I also remove your glove, you'll find my skin will warm yours even more. May I?" When she wordlessly passed her hand to him, he neatly peeled off her glove. While she sat watching his outline, he edged her elbow across his chest and took the palm of her hand to beneath the neckline of his waistcoat.

She should have been reluctant to accept this intimacy but the cold tended to wear down her resistance. Turning into him, she said, "I hope you're not trying to seduce me."

"I could think of a dozen ways to seduce you other than keeping your hand warm beneath my clothing. Would you rather keep your hands to yourself?"

"No. I would rather be in a nice warm drawing room."

He put his arm around her shoulders settled her more comfortably against his chest. "You will be soon. And then you will go back to Surrey to work on your garden and I will be trying to find another woman who would suit me as well as you."

She heaved a sigh, but with her arm across his chest, his words spoken into the top of her hair, she didn't feel as impartial as she could have hoped. "I don't know why you assume I would suit you. You hardly know me and we shouldn't be having this conversation while was are locked up together."

"Possibly but this might be my only chance with you."

"You don't want me. You really don't. I'm not the type of woman you are accustomed to." Her last words clogged in her throat. A duke wanted her. Perhaps not for the right reasons, and perhaps not the right way, but at least he had singled her out for his reprehensible attention.

At home, she was the sixth wheel. Being supplanted by Nora had been the last thing she had expected, despite the fact that she was pleased Papa had found a new wife.

However, she had been left without her accustomed role. Now Nora had a son, Cassia had to share her inheritance with another, if not lose the lot. She took her hand back and covered her eyes, holding back the threat of tears.

He took her hands from her face and gave her a length of cloth. "Use my cravat if you need to wipe your eyes."

"Thank you," she said, her voice husky. "But I'm not crying."

"That's good to know. If I have to keep dispensing with clothes, you'll have me naked soon." His voice held a certain amount of rueful charm.

She placed his cravat around her own neck and tucked the ends into her cleavage, adding a little more warmth to the bare area. When she had stopped wriggling, he put his arm around her shoulder and leaned her back against his side.

Her head found a comfortable place beneath his chin. Amazingly, she settled against him. His hand smoothed over her hair. One of her clips snagged in his shirtsleeve and was lost in the darkness. Half her hair fell to her shoulders. Too dispirited too care, she brought her other arm around and rested her hand on the front of his wide chest, leaving her snuggled right into him. His heart beat beneath her palm, a somewhat comforting reality. "I feel as though I have no one left now that Papa has Nora and her sons." His waistcoat muffled her voice.

"Yet, if you had married and he hadn't, he would feel the same way about you."

"I would live close by. I would only be a few miles away."

"You're still set on marrying George." He sighed and his

hand stilled on the back of her neck. His thumb idly rubbed her skin in a comforting way. "I don't think he plans to marry for years. In fact, he told me so only today."

She raised her face but in the dark she couldn't make out his features other than the vague outline. "I can't very well ask him to marry me right away simply because my father married."

"Ask me. I will marry you."

She gave a wry smile, lost in the black of the night, almost tempted to ask so that she could watch how quickly he backed out. "It would serve you right if I did, but I'm not about to ask anyone to marry me." She pushed herself upright. "What do you think the time is now?"

"No idea, but I can't hear any music. All I can hear are the night birds."

"So, someone will come looking soon. I had best put my gloves back on." She thought of returning his cravat but she appreciated the warmth too much to make a useless gesture. "I'm sorry I made a mess of your clothes. I'm sure we can smooth out your cravat well enough when you need it."

"We?"

"Can you put it on without a mirror?"

"Probably. I don't mind how I look because I don't have the same faith as you that anyone will search for me. I think my coachman will take Jeremy home and Jeremy will assume I went elsewhere."

"Is that the sort of thing you would normally do?"

"I have been known to spend the night gambling. What will your father assume?"

"I don't know. I've always been where I should be. I think he will worry and look for me."

"No one will worry about me unless I don't turn up for the cricket match in the morning. Let's hope, shall we? In the meantime, close your eyes. You can lean on me as long as you like. I'm not going anywhere without you and if we have to wait, we may as well rest."

Apparently, she had added being a dead bore to her list of faults. For a while she sat upright, trying to fix her hair in a rudimentary way. He seemed to be breathing rhythmically. She didn't doubt for one minute that he had fallen asleep. The amount of times her father had nodded off in the carriage while travelling was legendary. Men seemed to have that skill whereas she had never been able to sleep sitting up.

The wind hushed outside and the chinks of light through the doorway brightened. With her slowly acquired night vision she saw Huntsdale sleeping with his chin on his chest. His profile was magnificent with his strong nose and jaw making a silhouette anyone would see as heroic on a cameo. One lock of his dark hair had fallen across his forehead. The urge to reach out and smooth his wave back almost overtook her but instead she slipped off her shoes and brought her knees up under her skirts. She had been warmer close to him but she still had his jacket, into which she snuggled her arms. Her eyes closed. Sometime later, she realized she had warm but hard pillow beneath her head.

When she next opened her eyes, bright morning light streamed in from the doorway. "My Lord Duke. Is that you?" The voice sounded surprised.

She squinted against the light at the ginger-whiskered

man wearing a calico shirt and rough cotton breeches, who stood framed by daylight. His clothes identified him as a stable hand. Blinking, she lifted her head from Huntsdale's knees.

Huntsdale slowly opened his eyes. "Good morning, Mulligan. Good morning Miss Lacey."

She sat up and checked her hair. "We fell asleep," she said to the stable hand, somewhat dazed. "I can't believe it."

Huntsdale shifted his focus from her to Mulligan. "The door slammed on us last night. Now we're in a pickle. Would you harness up Sir Waldo's gig and drive us home."

Mulligan blinked at him. "Not unless Sir Waldo says. And the lady? She might not like to be seen dressed like that in an open conveyance so early in the morning."

"Oh, I certainly don't want to be transported through the streets like this," Cassia said, aghast. She whipped off Huntsdale's cravat and tried to pass it to him.

Huntsdale stretched, staring at her. "I'll go up the house and rouse Sir Waldo, then." This morning he looked like a stranger, large, rumpled and far too handsome with his hair mussed and his shirt half out of his breeches. "What's the time?"

"Nigh on seven. Sir Waldo has already finished breakfast. He don't stay abed all day." Mulligan backed. "I'll ask him. He's in the stables next door seeing to the carriage for church."

"I'm right here." Sir Waldo, a head shorter than Mulligan, appeared behind him. "Morning, Adam. Got stuck into the brandy last night, did you? Jeremy wondered where you went. And, oh my lord, Miss Lacey." He took a step back, his mouth a perfect oval of surprise. "Now what's to do?"

Cassia held her breath. At best she would appear foolish. At worst she would appear as disreputable as she looked, with her hair hanging down her back, Huntsdale's jacket dwarfing her, and his cravat hanging from her hold. "I'm afraid that I ran in here last night when the rain came. And the door slammed shut."

"I raced in behind her," Huntsdale said, reaching to take his cravat, his gaze meeting hers. "And we were shut in together."

"Were you now?" Sir Waldo drew down his eyebrows and shot an accusing glare at Huntsdale, before he glanced at Cassia. "Perhaps you would like to freshen up in the house, Miss Lacey?"

Cassia would rather die. She wished the ground would open up and swallow her. "I think the sooner I set my parents' mind at ease, the better."

"I expect they were surprised to find you hadn't taken a hackney home, as they thought," Sir Waldo said, politely.

Huntsdale slung his crumpled cravat around his neck. "I shall see your parents with you and explain what happened."

The man looked outrageously masculine when half dressed and unshaven. She had never particularly enjoyed the sight of a stubbled chin, but seeing him as a man rather than a rich society lay-about had a warming affect on her blood. For once, he wasn't groomed to perfection. She wanted to smile at him, but she suspected she ought to appear relieved to be rescued rather than admiring of her co-prisoner. "Thank you, but I think I will do far better without you."

"I think Miss Lacey could do with a cup of coffee. I'll take her to my wife." Yet again, Sir Waldo shot a glare at Huntsdale. "I'm sure she would like to freshen up before she returns home."

"We were locked in, Sir Waldo." Cassia swallowed. "Or we wouldn't have spent the night. We couldn't dislodge the door, or find a nail or anything else to use to lift the bar."

"That's strange. Normally it's as loose as a gossip's tongue." Sir Waldo rubbed his hair and stood back, and indicated the way to the main house. "I'll be back in a moment to discuss whatever needs to be discussed with you," he said in a dire tone to Adam.

"Shouldn't I be discussing whatever needs to be discussed, too? I feel so awful about this and I must apologize. I meant to walk around the garden to clear my head and the rain took me unaware."

"I was worried about her when I saw her leave, and so I followed her." Huntsdale watched her face.

She stared back at him, wondering what had worried him about her. "You had no need, and you shouldn't have. If you hadn't, you wouldn't have been locked in with me." She struggled out of his jacket, which she passed to him.

Sir Waldo patted her hand. He gave Huntsdale a quelling glance. "I'm not quite certain what is to be done, but Lady Gerard will know. Wait here for me, Adam." Taking Cassia's arm, he guided her toward the house.

Lady Gerard coped rather well when she discovered where Cassia had spent the night. She simply sat Cassia at the dining room table and rang the bell for a maid.

"I do feel dreadful about this, Lady Gerard." Cassia's hair slid across her back. Strands of straw had caught in her gown and she doubtless looked a mess. "I don't normally inspect other people's outbuildings at night, but the ball … I'm not used to polite society and going to balls night after night. I wanted to clear my head."

"I don't know what your father and stepmother will say to me, not noticing that one of our guests was locked in our feed shed all night long." Lady Gerard paused to tell the maid to bring a pot of coffee and bread and butter. When the girl had left the room, she turned again to Cassia. "We don't want any unnecessary gossip. Drink your coffee, dear, and I'll find the girls and get them on their way to church."

With no other choice, Cassia sat drinking coffee in her crushed ball gown, chastened and solitary in her embarrassment. If she had a friend, she would have someone with whom to discuss her confusion. She wouldn't dream of sharing her thoughts with Papa or Nora, who these days seemed to be a single unit.

Once Cassia had a close friend, but she had left the district when Cassia was thirteen. After that, Cassia had a governess who listened to her, but she left to marry. Then Cassia's mother died. Since then, she hadn't formed a close relationship with anyone. She simply didn't want to become too attached. The idea of being constantly deserted had convinced her she needed to learn how to stand alone, and until now she had managed quite well.

And she would manage quite well again. She drew a breath long enough to straighten her spine and raise her chin. Whatever had to be done, she would do.

Chapter Six

"So, you were locked in, were you?" Sir Waldo glared at Adam.

"Yes, sir, we were." Adam squared his shoulders.

Sir Waldo narrowed his eyes. "And how do you think you were locked in?"

"The bar wedged itself. Perhaps the hinge had rusted."

"If indeed that is so, you will still have to consider Miss Lacey," Sir Waldo said, his military moustache twitching. "She is a respectable woman from a good family. She can't have her reputation destroyed."

Bertie Gerard suddenly appeared around the corner of the feed shed. When he saw Huntsdale, he widened his eyes with surprise. "Adam! Good God, man. Why are you still here?" Bertie wore his Sunday best with a tall black hat shading his cherubic round face. He had inherited his parents' lack of height, and his mother's fair coloring.

Sir Waldo turned his face skyward and raised his hands, as if asking the heavens to give him an answer. "Adam spent the night in the feed shed with Miss Lacey." He narrowed his eyes. His voice deadly with meaning, he said, "The door was locked."

Bertie's jaw dropped. "Locked? You know where we keep the lifter," he said to Adam.

"The lifter was missing."

His sandy eyebrows lowered, Sir Waldo turned to his son. "Do you know anything about this?"

Bertie stared at his feet, and short of shuffling, he couldn't have looked more abashed. "About the bar-lifter, nothing. Lucien told me that he saw Adam run in after Cassia Lacey and he thought it might be helpful to shut the door."

"Helpful? In what way would that be helpful if he couldn't get out? If anyone finds out about this, the gossips will slaughter Miss Lacey." Sir Waldo poked his son in the chest with one hard finger. "You and your foolish friends will keep this quiet."

Bertie shook his head, not as a negative but as if trying to settle his brain. "Of course, we will keep this quiet. If I hadn't thought Adam could move the bar, I would never have left him all night."

"I thought I could," Adam said, frowning. "When I couldn't find the lifter, I shook the damned door but the bar was fixed. Try for yourself."

Clearly no one believed Adam. Bertie let down the bar and tried rattling the door himself. He turned as pale as uncooked pastry. "You're right. I can't apologize enough."

"You certainly can't, my lad." Sir Waldo's lips pressed together and he stared with a modicum of sympathy at Adam. "Are you prepared to marry Miss Lacey?"

"I am." Adam straightened his stance and folded his arms across his chest.

"So, we played right into your hands, didn't we?" Bertie said bitterly. "And not for the first time."

"This would be the first time that one of Lucien's pranks backfired without the outcome being a great disappointment." Raising his chin, Adam stared down at his too helpful friend. "I suggest that neither of you speak about this again."

Bertie's mouth drooped. "Of course we won't." Head down, he swung on his heels, and began heading back to the house.

"Remember, don't say a word about this," his father called after him. He tugged his ear lobe, staring at the newly swept cobblestones beneath his feet. "This is one of those occasions when the truth won't be a scrap of use. Let us hope that her parents accept your story."

Adam shrugged, quite sure of the outcome. "They brought her to town to find a husband. As a gentleman, I certainly intend to right the wrong done to her and make her an offer. The Laceys would be foolish to refuse a title for their daughter."

"The Laceys are respectable country folk. A duke might be a little much for them."

Adam began tying his cravat, ignoring Sir Waldo's words. "I see no reason why she should refuse me. Let's face it. If we count Lucien, at least five people know I spent the night with her in your shed. The story is sure to leak out at some stage." As far as he was concerned, the outcome was clear.

In fact, the whole situation couldn't be been better had

the locking of the door been planned. Of course, when he had told Lucien he wanted to be left alone with Cassia, he hadn't meant he wanted to be locked up with her, but Lucien wasn't to know that the latch-lifter was missing. And since Adam had wanted Cassia from the start and now he had her, he couldn't possibly rail at Lucien's childish prank.

As for Cassia's feelings, even this morning, after she'd had an uncomfortable sleep, she hadn't focused on the locked door or how the problem had eventuated. She accepted that what was done, was done, and they both needed to make best of the situation. What better way than marrying the woman whose first smile had lifted his heart?

He had always known he would inherit the dukedom, but until he had done so, he hadn't been aware that he would have no other life. A responsibility shared was a responsibility halved, and who better to share with than a woman who knew how to manage? Aside from that, she had sense. She didn't giggle and try to charm him. She simply spoke to him as if he was a man and not a duke. When she wasn't trying to fight him off, she appeared to enjoy his company, too. She showed this by the tilt of her generous mouth, and the gleam in her clever eyes. Her company relaxed him. During the first hour after meeting her he had known that Cassia was the woman for him.

Love was a subject about which he was ignorant. By all accounts, his father had thought he loved Adam's mother before he married her. Adam, however, had no memories of love in the family home. His parents fought the whole time. His mother flew off the handle whenever she was crossed and the house had always been filled with strife and noise.

Cassia was cool and calm. Even when Huntsdale displeased her, she didn't make a fuss. She simply said what she thought and left him in no doubt that if he applied logic, she would hear the sense in his words. Most other young ladies pretended to agree with him, which he found needless. Hearing other opinions than his own stimulated him. He had been know to change his mind—although now he came to think of it, he couldn't recall the last time this had happened.

" ... staff and probably, by now, also the indoor staff." Sir Waldo frowned at him. "Are you listening to me, Adam? You will be lucky if none of this tale leaks out. The main problem is that you were both missing at the same time. By now, more than a few people would have added one and one."

"I'll keep that in mind to tell her parents. Now, could you send someone over to my house? I would like the landau brought here to transport Cassia home."

"I wish you luck, Adam." Sir Waldo pulled on his gloves. "You may well be thought of as some sort of hero, since the situation is not your fault. I dread to think Beatrice would have acted in such a situation." He shivered with faked apprehension. "I am quite sure that she would have had more to say than *'thank you, Waldo. Of course I will marry you.'*"

Adam almost smiled as he trudged up to the house with Sir Waldo. Before the man had married his dear wife, he had been a major in the British army. Adam was one of the richest men in London. Cassia's parents would more than likely snap up a wealthy duke in a trice.

The triumphant shrieking calls from a flock of gray geese supported his stance.

~

Never before had Cassia been so humiliated. Without a doubt she looked dreadful with her hair hastily re-knotted and her shoulders covered by Lady Gerard's short woolen cape. Expanding her lungs deeply enough to lift her shoulders, she used the black iron knocker on the door of the Lacey's hired house.

She had barely spoken a word to Huntsdale during the short trip in his luxurious landau. Instead she had stared at the rigid back of the uniformed driver who clipped the vehicle along at a smart pace through the deserted streets. What the man may have thought of her, she would doubtless never know, but she knew what she thought of herself. She could barely hold up her head.

Having to be kept hidden away in the dining room from the Gerard sisters had set the tone for her. Despite the situation only being half her fault, she was to blame for causing a flurry in at least one household. The second, hers, would be sure to follow suit.

Clearly unprepared for a visitor so early in the morning, the housekeeper creaked open the door of the hired house. "Miss Lacey? Your ma and pa have been up all night worrying about you. Barely a few hours ago, your ma …" Her voice petered out as she spotted Huntsdale. Although the crease between her eyebrows said she didn't know Cassia's escort, even she could see by the spanking new landau attached to the pair of high-bred chestnuts that stood not twelve feet away, that the gentleman by Cassia's side was an important personage.

Cassia wasn't, but a housekeeper had no right to judge her employer's daughter by her bedraggled state. "Thank you, Mrs. Riley. If you will, tell Lady Lacey I have arrived home safely."

Mrs. Riley stepped back, turned, and proceeded at her own pace up the stairs.

Cassia glanced at Huntsdale. "Thank you for your escort, sir. I'll go inside now." She held her hand out for him to shake.

He ignored the gesture, using a firm smile. "I think I should explain the situation to your parents."

"I really think your presence would not be helpful." She stepped inside and he followed before she could shut the door on him.

She gave him the kind of stare she used on the head-gardener when he tried to get the better of her, but he ignored that too. With no other choice, she showed her chivalrous knight into the shabby sitting room. Although he hadn't yet shaved, he didn't look particularly untidy. Like Cassia, he still wore his evening clothes but he took off his hat as he turned to stare out the window.

Nora arrived first, her hair scooped back into a hasty roll and her brown gown one of those she would wear at home for visitors. Her face looked pale and her expression wary. She rushed at Cassia and hugged her. "We had no idea where you had gone," she said in a worried voice. "It seemed some mischief was afoot. Your father has been awaiting a ransom note." She gave a high-pitched, half-hysterical laugh.

Papa stepped into the doorway, his shirt barely tucked into his trousers and his cravat hanging from under his collar. His gaze assessed the situation. He walked toward Huntsdale holding out his hand. "I assume I have you to thank for her rescue," he said, his voice hoarse.

Huntsdale clasped Papa's one hand between his two. "Not at all. I was glad to be of service. All is well. Sir Waldo's groom found us this morning locked in his feed shed." Although his confident posture had annoyed Cassia previously, in this situation she was glad he could remain confident.

"Locked in his feed shed?" Papa dropped Huntsdale's hold. He stared at Cassia, his eyebrows almost hitting his hairline.

"Accidently," Cassia said, her voice inexplicably shaking. "The wind blew the door shut and the lock activated. We couldn't open it."

"We? Us?" Pa's voice rose higher.

Cassia glanced at her hands. She had hoped not to have to mention Huntsdale and she wished he hadn't mentioned himself. "The duke followed me in." She met Papa's gaze. "The rain began to pour and at the time, the shed seemed like a good place to shelter."

"He followed you? Then you spent the night in a shed together?" Papa moved over to the moth-eaten fainting couch and sat, his head in his hands. "Who else knows about this?"

"Sir Waldo and Lady Gerard." Cassia stood proudly. She would not have her morals doubted by her own family.

Huntsdale cleared his throat. "Bertie Gerard too. And the outdoor servants. Possibly the indoor servants as well.

Cassia went inside the house for a cup of coffee this morning."

Papa raised his head, his expression bleak. "I'm ashamed of you, Cassia. Do you imagine you are some kind of housemaid? Surely you could have ... you trysted with him in a shed? I can scarcely believe this of my own daughter."

"I didn't tryst, Papa." Cassia blinked hard. "It was coincidental. I had no idea he was behind me."

"Were you not attending a ball?" Papa's expression turned from disappointment to severity. "Why should you find a need to go outside?"

Cassia twisted her hands together. "It wasn't raining when I left the ballroom. I wanted to clear my head. That's all. If I had wanted to talk to the duke I would have, but I didn't, and so I didn't. Talk to him. Not in the ballroom. Or not for long." She swallowed.

She had wanted to talk to him in the feed shed. His proximity, the darkness, and the intimacy of the entire situation made her see the duke in a completely different way. Now the very thought of him made her breath catch. He had been her protector, her refuge. A woman who had largely been independent, she didn't imagine finding comfort while in circumstances beyond her control. He hadn't turned away from her in the morning. He had smiled at her as if he honestly liked her. In one single night, he had changed from a disreputable friend of George's into a wildly attractive male, which had been her first impression of him those few weeks ago in Surrey.

"So, he forced you to go outside with him?"

Her neck stiffened. "He forced me? Of course he didn't. I left the ballroom alone. We stepped into the shed together, and the door swung closed. The duke tried to open it but he discovered the lock had jammed. He kindly gave up his jacket for me so that I could be comfortable. He couldn't have been more courteous if he had tried. And I suspect he tried because the situation was extremely awkward, as you must be aware."

Papa ran his hand through his hair, leaving gray strands standing in the air. "And you say the Gerards' staff know about this?" His eyes narrowed, he scrutinized the expression on Huntsdale's face.

Huntsdale didn't appear phased at all. "They're not likely to say a word, sir, and I doubt the few members of the family Gerard who know the situation will speak of this again." He offered a wry shrug. "Sir Patrick said you searched for quite a while."

Papa shook his head, his eyebrows drawn together. "Clearly, glancing in the feed shed didn't occur to any of us. Now my daughter's reputation is at stake. And if the younger gentleman find out about this, they're exactly the people who shouldn't be suspicious of my daughter's character if she is to find a husband while we're in the city."

"I don't care what anyone thinks of me, Papa," Cassia said in a constricted voice. She cleared her throat. "I'm not planning to marry just yet." Her last few words didn't seem as easy to say today as yesterday. George would not like to know that she had spent a night with Huntsdale, a friend of his or not.

Papa shook his head. "You go upstairs and refresh yourself, Cassia. I'll handle this."

"There's nothing to handle. I won't be heartbroken if I can't go to any more balls, or even if we have go back home sooner than expected." Cassia raised her chin, despite the solitariness of her position.

Her father stared at her without speaking. Nora made a sympathetic face and gave a significant glance at the door. Without appearing unbecomingly defiant, Cassia couldn't stay when she had been told to leave. Her chest aching, she turned to the duke, forced a smile, and made a half curtsey. "Thank you for your kindness toward me, sir. I can't deny that I need a change of clothes and a wash. And of course, you will want to leave for church." She held her head high as she left the completely silent room. She had reached the stairs before she heard a low-voiced conversation begin again.

In her tiny room, she sat on the edge of her bed in a huddled heap, staring at her face in the dressing table mirror, not recognizing the expression of defeat she saw. She dragged in a breath, blinking hard. No matter what life served her, she would not allow herself to be shamed. With aching slowness, she stood. With one flick, she removed Lady Gerard's cape and then she reached for her hairbrush. A woman wearing a bird's nest on her head could not wage a war on public opinion.

Slowly, she removed her hairclips, counting each. She had lost five. No matter. She rang for a maid. Hobson, appeared, her hands in an anxious clasp.

"I need you to unhook me, if you will, Hobson."

The maid came into the room, her expression deliberately blank. Apparently Cassia's disgrace had already been discussed downstairs. Hobson didn't speak a word as she unhooked Cassia's bodice and untied her skirts and petticoats. She even folded the garments neatly and placed them in Cassia's trunk at the foot of the bed, while Cassia donned her dressing robe. Finally she said, "I'll bring your water, Miss."

Wearing nothing but a robe over her underclothes, Cassia ran the brush through her long hair one hundred times. The hot water arrived, and she washed. Although she knew neither her nor Huntsdale's behavior had been reprehensible, she could understand that others might think so. Given time, the affair would be nothing more than a shrug in her memory. Until then, she had to hold her head high—or leave for home.

Finally she heard the front door shut and the landau drive off. A light rap sounded on her door. Nora popped her head in. "Your father wants to speak to you in the sitting room."

Cassia heaved a sigh. "I'll need to dress. I'll be there as soon as I can." She put on her pink morning gown. She had expected to attend the weekly cricket match the duke had mentioned, but she doubted she would be allowed out until Papa came to his senses. When she had also tidied her hair, she went down again, not at all sure she would be contrite when she had heard more than enough chiding than she deserved already.

Papa stood staring out of the window. "Sit down."

She did so, and he turned to face her, his hands clasped behind his back. "I'm sure you won't be surprised to know that your season is over."

A pang of wretchedness shot through her. "I had no idea that everyone would make such a fuss. It looks bad, but surely if we simply smile and ignore the whole thing, everyone else will, too?"

He shook his head. "I don't intend to take a shamed daughter back home in disgrace. Your mother, had she lived, would have been most disappointed in you, and she would be even more disappointed in me if I didn't make sure Huntsdale would do the right thing. Fortunately, he agreed to marry you. He very courteously asked me for your hand."

"He, of all people, knows he has no need." Her voice pitched a little too high, making her sound more like a twittering fool than a woman refusing a proposal of marriage.

"Apparently not. He agrees that the sooner, the better. Before anyone has a chance to gossip about you, he will make known his intentions. He thought he should begin by announcing your betrothal today at the cricket match." His gaze met hers.

Cassia's cheeks froze. "Did either of you consider asking my permission?"

Lines of impatience formed between Papa's eyebrows. "Last night you noticeably disappeared during a ball. Huntsdale did the same. People need to be told some sort of tale, or gossip will begin connecting the two events. The story we plan to tell is that you had a raging headache and Huntsdale took you home in his carriage so that he wouldn't spoil our enjoyment. And that we found you here. He will tell the same story."

Cassia closed her eyes momentarily. This morning she had been confronted with Sir Waldo's suspicion, Lady Gerard's worrying, Huntsdale's kindness, and Papa's righteousness. Too much had happened. Too many people wanted to interfere in her life, and too many people had indicated that she was a problem. After a life of unthinking respectability, she was now learning no one was above suspicion. Her head whirled. She supposed she was tired. She had no idea what to do for the best.

The worst part had been her behavior. She should never have left the ball. Instead, she should have joined the other young ladies without dancing partners and discussed all the young men with prospects, as if she could pick and choose where she would. Those discussions never appealed to her because the end result, marriage, would make her a chattel. George understood her. He wouldn't treat her that way.

If she agreed to the duke's proposal, she would lose the autonomy granted to her by her father. However, Huntsdale's behavior toward her in their trying situation had been impeccable. His touch had been reassuring. She'd felt no qualms about snuggling into him. The man had a large comfortable chest. She could no longer see him as a stranger, especially when he'd said she could ask him to marry her. She had heard his words as amusing nonsense. Now she worried that she had hinted an expectation she did not hold. She had completely misjudged the man.

If she had to marry someone, and she could choose by inspecting a long line, her choice would doubtless linger over him. His behavior had been truly noble.

Adam smacked at the ball with his willow bat. The ball sailed high to the boundary. "Six!" yelled his team in a chorus. He waited for the fielders to send the ball back to the bowler.

Cassia hadn't arrived yet. Last night, she had been easy

on him. He appreciated her calmness. He liked that she didn't make a fuss once she realized that she would have to spend the night in the feed shed with him. Keeping his hands off her had been torture but he had enough sense to know that a vulnerable woman would prefer a man to protect her than attempt to seduce her.

He had hopes that she would learn to appreciate him. After all, they had a friendship of sorts. Once she became accustomed to the idea of being his wife, she would realize he wasn't a harsh man, and he could be generous.

As long as she didn't disrupt his usual routine, they would get along splendidly. Being a managing sort of woman, she would easily deal with his staff. She'd had practice running a house before her father remarried. Women who could cope without constant questioning, and she was clearly one, were the types he preferred.

He fronted up to the wicket again, remembering how well she had organized George's country picnic. And now this paragon of efficiency was promised to him. He would enjoy continuing to change her mind about him. Last night she had relaxed in his arms. While she had slept on his lap, she had unknowingly placed her hands on his lower abdomen. Despite the fact that her touch had been unconscious, he had still reacted with indrawn breath. Because he was a gentleman he had removed said hands.

He laughed to himself because that wasn't quite true. A certain body part had been overjoyed, and if she had awoken she might not have been equally so. Best he protected his reputation as a gentleman when he wanted her to appreciate that until they'd left the feed shed, he hadn't taken advantage of the situation, or at least, not that way.

The bowler ran up, his expression ferocious. Adam's own expression was resigned and, without any effort, he shot the next hit to the boundary. At least his poor night's sleep hadn't put him off his game. A slight ruffle in the crowds caused him to focus in that direction. Ah, the family Lacey had arrived. He could let himself be taken out now. Facing the bowler again, he waited, but the fool went wide of the wicket. Someone like Lucien would have him out in a second, but Lucien was on Adam's team, and standing among the crowd. He hit the next shot into a fielder who dropped the ball while Huntsdale made two reluctant runs. With his next hit, he was finally run out. Relieved, he stripped off his gloves as he walked over to the large group of friends and relatives of his team. The Lacey family lingered among them.

"I hope you will accept my apology for last night." Lucien separated himself from the crowd, his expression wary as he watched Huntsdale unbuckle his leg pads.

"What's done is done." Adam lifted his eyebrows. "You'll keep the matter quiet, I know."

"Naturally. There is nothing I can say that won't make the situation worse. The lady is looking your way."

"I'd best make myself presentable, in that case."

He unbuckled the pads, leaving them resting against the boundary fence. His team wore burgundy cravats for unity. He brushed down his breeches, found his jacket in the team area, and strolled across to the Lacey family.

Until she turned, he didn't notice Amelia, who stood beside Lady Gerard.

He stepped back in shock. The auburn haired beauty acknowledged him with a slight inclination of her head. Best to pretend not to recognize her. Forcing all expression from his face, he managed to keep moving. He couldn't imagine what she might be doing at a cricket match or who on earth would have introduced her to Lady Gerard. A less suitable acquaintance for a leader of society, he couldn't imagine.

He reached Cassia with a smile he didn't contain. "Miss Lacey." He couldn't account for the relief he experienced when she offered a rueful shrug of her shoulders.

"Your Grace. I must thank you again for sending me home in your carriage last night. I hear that everyone thought I was missing."

He blinked. "You went home in my carriage?"

"Surely you remember offering me the use of it?"

"If you say I did, then I did." He glanced around, nodding at her father and her stepmother who stood beside her. The story's embellishment was new to him but perhaps established some sort of relationship between them. "Did you manage to repair the rip in your gown?"

"Not yet, sir. If you recall, I had a headache."

He laughed softly. Anyone close enough to hear would have no idea what to make of this conversation. "We must get our story straight or people will think that possibly we left early together."

She glanced at him, her cool blue eyes overlarge, leaving the rest to him.

He obliged, fixing his gaze on Lady Gerard, who stood closest, between her daughters and her husband. "We did, of course, but I'm sure we can be forgiven. I wanted to ask Sir Robert and Lady Lacey for Cassia's hand in marriage."

The Gerard girls turned to each other, eyes widened with surprise. "We are all so pleased to hear that," Lady Gerard said, letting out a relieved sigh.

"Well done." Sir Waldo pounded him on the shoulder. "Well done. And best wishes to you, Miss Lacey. I wish you luck with this man, though I don't doubt he will make a splendid husband."

"Let's hope I make a splendid wife," Cassia muttered just loud enough for him to hear. "Thank you everyone for your good wishes. Now, I believe we came here for a cricket match."

"This is far better entertainment, isn't it Mama?" Daisy Gerard, a girl of sixteen and the youngest of the bunch, looked utterly delighted. "I didn't expect the duke to marry until he was very old."

Since he was twelve years older than she, he found a stern gaze. "I expect that's your way of congratulating me."

"Of course, duke, though I can't say I approve of marriage."

"When the time comes for you, you will," her mother said, trying to look fond instead of exasperated. Daisy, Jeremy's favorite of the Gerard girls was a born pest, which he enjoyed, being an irresponsible charmer himself. He liked to bait her and she rose beautifully.

Today, Adam didn't intend to let Daisy distract him. However, Amelia moved to stand beside Lady Gerard, who smiled at her. "Cassia, have you met Mrs. Gates?"

"I have not had that pleasure." Cassia smiled politely.

Amelia glanced quickly at him before speaking. "How

do you do, Miss Lacey?" The merry widow had a pink spot high on each cheekbone as she shook Cassia's hand.

Huntsdale wanted to ask her to move along but if he did, he would make a spectacle of them both. He raised his eyebrows at her. "We do well, Mrs. Gates. What brings you to the cricket?"

She took the hint. Smart woman, Mrs. Gates. "Although I should not take this as an opportunity to promote myself, I will say that I am delighted to be here and to meet Miss Lacey. You would not know, your grace, but I have recently set up as a wardrobe coordinator, as it were, for the young ladies wishing to make a mark in society."

Cassia appeared pleased with this. "It would make life so much easier to know someone with style who is willing to impart her knowledge. I have a gown or two I am not quite sure about."

Adam concentrated on Cassia. Today, she wore a gown in a stark shade of blue with multilayered frills making a gushing waterfall of the neck and a filling lake at the bottom of the skirts. Perhaps she thought adding twice the needed fabric to each gown would make her appear more stylish. Perhaps if she added less … a thought that caused him to draw a deep breath. "Should we presume one you are not sure about is your white lace ball gown?" And then he could have kicked himself for he certainly didn't want the two women put together.

Cassia smiled. "That gown cost Papa a fortune. Though I expect half of it would make a very fine gown."

"I would be delighted to advise you, Miss Lacey." Amelia demurely lowered her lashes.

"What do you think, Nora?" Cassia turned to her stepmother.

Lady Lacey had been watching Cassia closely. She gave a tiny start and glanced at Sir Robert. "As to that, the gown was made by a country seamstress. If it needs a few changes, I would say that ..."

"Thank you, Mrs. Gates. I shall make an appointment to see you," Cassia said firmly, clearly having made her own decision about the gown.

Amelia smiled politely. "No doubt, bearing in mind the announcement of your betrothal, you will want a trousseau, too?"

"Not instantly." Cassia began to fiddle with the button on her sleeve. "I doubt I will marry for a year or so."

Lady Lacey glanced at her in horror. Adam glanced at Lady Lacey. He had said he would marry Cassia as soon as possible, and he had decided he would not wait. Cedric Rogers, his secretary, could arrange the matter tomorrow.

"Given the choice between sooner or later, I will take sooner," Adam said, picking up Cassia's hand. Last night, she had given him the impression that she could abide him. She had trusted him not to take advantage of a situation not of her making, and he had lived up to her expectations. When he had held her in his arms, he held her honor and her trust. He had no intention of waiting now he had her promise.

The quick blinking and the slight tinge of pink on her cheeks said she was embarrassed. "I'm not in any hurry."

He understood that she needed to convey a message about her lack of guilt to the few people who knew that he and she had been together overnight. "Nor should you be, my dear, but I am." He snatched her into his arms and swung her around in a circle, a teasing smile on his face. Her skirts landed a little after her feet.

After staring deep into her questioning eyes, he slowly lowered his head and lightly kissed her. Being in the centre of a rapidly growing crowd meant he needed to be circumspect, but the softness of her lips and the fresh clean smell of her closed his eyes with appreciation.

"Whenever you say," her lovely, obstinate mouth said, as her hands pushed against his shoulders. "For I would dearly love to stop being the day's entertainment."

Chapter Seven

Adam hovered in the doorway of his secretary's private abode, a set of rooms on the third floor of the Huntsdale town house. "I have an urgent job for you."

Cedric raised his bespectacled gaze from the ledger opened on his lap. Beside him, a scone surrounded by a blot of jam and cream waited to be consumed. "Your wish is my command." A smile wrinkled the corners of his eyes as he closed the pages.

"I want you to arrange for the banns to be called so that I can marry. As soon as you have, book a wedding at St. Luke's church for some time during the next three weeks."

"A wedding?" Cedric lowered his head and peered at Adam over the top of his reading glasses. "For anyone we know?"

Adam stood perfectly still, his shoulders squared, blinking at Cedric. "Miss Cassia Lacey has consented to be my bride." A niggle of uncertainty caused him to curl his fingers into his palms. He had let himself be known as the hero of the piece, when he knew he was nothing but an opportunist.

"Congratulations, your grace. That is wonderful news, indeed." Cedric managed a discreet cough. "But may I remind you that today is Sunday?"

Adam nodded. The idea of Cassia having time to rethink caused him an amount of apprehension. He rested his hand on the doorknob. "Which makes today the one day of the week that we can be sure the church is open. You won't have any problems. I'm willing to speed the matter with a hefty donation to the vicar and I'm not fussy as to the date. I don't want to waste any time on this now the decision is made."

"Will your lovely affianced have time to manage what she needs to do on her end within three weeks—new gowns, a trousseau? Who will plan the reception?"

"You will do so, old chap. She won't need a trousseau. She can buy whatever she needs after we are married. Draw up an agreement for her allowance, too, while you're at it."

Cedric plastered each half of his scone with jam and cream. "I see I won't have a moment to spare." He pushed the two halves together, took one enormous bite, and rose to his feet.

"Nor will I." Adam pulled down the cuffs of his jacket, prepared to get on with his paperwork. "I'm sure that parading Miss Lacey around her social events will keep me busy."

Cedric hastily chewed and swallowed. "If you are planning on paying for her tardy trousseau, I imagine I'll need to take out an account with dressmakers and milliners. Are you planning on making a visit to the bank?" He bit off the second third of his scone.

"Am I short of money?"

"She may be short of jewelry. Your mother's is held in the bank."

Adam nodded, glad to be reminded. "Oh, and find someone to decorate the church. We'll hold the reception here. I imagine you'll have to organize that as well. Send invitations to everyone. We can't do this without a little ostentation."

"It's extremely short notice. You possibly won't get any of the royal dukes to come." Cedric pushed the last of his scone into his mouth and brushed the crumbs off the front of his shirt.

"I don't care who comes, old chap, as long as the bride appears. Let her family know today. They're sure to have a few arrangements to make, as well." Adam turned and strode back to his study. The arrangements for his marriage now settled, he could finally concentrate on his favorite place, his large country estate.

He was the fifth duke to occupy one of the largest manor houses in England. His father had restored the east wing, and Adam planned to restore the west wing, but first he wanted to experiment with his crops. The recent rotations between barley and sheep had invigorated the soil. He could now plant a larger area. This meant he needed more workers, who would have to be found outside his immediate area.

Intending to build more workers' cottages, he wrote a note to himself to arrange a meeting with the local mayor, for more shops would be needed in the village for the worker's families, who could also be employed. None of this could be done in three weeks.

In three weeks he would be married to a desirable woman who had experience in organizing households. If she could manage to put at least two of his residences in order, her support would help him to march forward instead of stamping on the same ground. He had inherited a fortune, but thus far, he hadn't spent his money to improve the local conditions. With the support of his new wife, he could make the changes he had expected his father to adopt.

Cassia dressed quickly and hurried down to breakfast. After Mr. Rogers had politely explained last night that he had booked St. Luke's church for a wedding to be performed as soon as the banns had been read, Nora had flown into panic. Papa had been surprised and pleased in that order. The quickly cobbled plan had been for the two women to spend the morning shopping.

Although Cassia needed to discuss her trousseau, Papa had already left for Whites, where he read his newspaper in the morning and get caught up on all the latest gossip from his cronies.

"Good morning, Cassia. Should I pour you a cup of coffee while I am holding the pot?" Nora smiled placidly.

"If you would. You sound calm, but I am not. The whole of my trousseau is at home. We'll need to have it sent to London." Cassia buttered her bread, while Nora filled her cup. In the corner of the room, Baby Jack was beginning to made wuffling sounds in his cradle. Soon he would begin squalling. Nora would need to attend him, and Cassie would be left to plan while she ate her breakfast in peace.

"Yes, dear. The housekeeper at home can pack for you. Don't worry, please."

"I'm not worrying but I don't have anything but day gowns to send for and I can't dash off on my honeymoon with the wardrobe I brought for a few short weeks stay in the city. I'll need more. I know money is tight, but you have Mrs. Gates' address. Should we see if she would help us?" Today, she wore her blue gown. Huntsdale had glanced more than once at the frills. Clearly, he didn't admire too many embellishments because he had also made that unhelpful joke about her white gown. She wished she had been born with style.

Nora nodded. Although she had brushed up on her social skills, she didn't have a flair for fashion, either. The daughter of a vicar, she knew how to bake bread, preserve fruit, and be a delightful wife and mother. "Let me find the nursery maid, and we'll call on Mrs. Gates." She bustled out into the kitchen.

Cassia passed a rattle to Jack and had to pacify him while waiting for Nora to return with the nursery maid. Finally, Cassia hurried up to her bedroom to ready herself for shopping. Quite a lot of Papa's money had been wasted on unflattering gowns, already. If she could refurbish her town outfits, she wouldn't have to be even more beholden to Huntsdale.

In almost no time, the old carriage that had been hired with the house stood in the street outside awaiting passengers. Cassia settled into a saggy seat whose green upholstery needed renewing. The sway-backed horses took a step backward before moving off. Mrs. Gates lived within the city mile. Given sturdy shoes, Cassia would rather walk. When Cassia walked, her ideas multiplied, not that she had a single idea about her gowns, which was the reason why she had accepted Nora's choices in the first place.

After a plodding journey along streets clogged with delivery carts and darting pedestrians, she sat in the tired vehicle in front of a row of redbrick terraced houses in Newington Green. Glancing at the genteel houses, Cassia lost her enthusiasm. She desperately hoped that Mrs. Gates would be away from home. Nothing could be more galling than being examined from head to toe and found wanting in style. At home, her gowns didn't make a difference to the way people saw her. She was Miss Lacey and respected, which was all she wanted. She would much prefer to be accepted for herself rather than for the depths of her Papa's pockets.

"Do you have a pencil?" Nora began pulling cards and notes, a teething ring, a handkerchief, a tin of lozenges, and a needle and thread card from her reticule. "If she isn't at home, we should leave a note."

Preferring leaving a note to a visit, Cassia offered her neat combination notebook and pencil. She also had visiting cards, which didn't help, as she had only her Surrey address. While the horses stood idly flicking their tails, the driver appeared to go into a snooze. Nora wrote something on the paper. "There," she said, when done. "Let's see if she is home first."

Cassia wanted to say, *"You go and I'll wait,"* but if the lady should be at home, Cassia would appear to be rudely anxious to leave. So, she climbed down, holding out her hand for Nora. The front door stood on the street. Pretty French lace curtains covered the window either side. A sharp knock brought padded footsteps. The door opened, and the gap widened.

Mrs. Gates' beautiful hair was scooped back from her face and worn high, revealing the lace edging the neckline of her gray gown. "How delightful to see you both, Mrs. and Miss Lacey. Please come inside." Her expression welcoming, she led Cassia and Nora through a narrow hall and into a smallish drawing room tastefully hung with heavy blue brocade curtains and muffled by a thick floral carpet.

Cassia sat on a lady's chair of dark blue velvet while Nora and Mrs. Gates occupied a gold velvet sofa, each eying each other with a touch of curiosity. Nora spoke first. "My stepdaughter will need gowns more suited to a married lady."

"And you want my advice as to the styles?" Mrs. Gates asked carefully.

"I want to be sure she looks her best. She is about to marry a duke." Nora widened her eyes at Cassia, silently begging her to speak.

"I have country-made gowns, Mrs. Gates. My stepmother wants me to look town smart." Cassia toyed with her reticule, trying not to examine Mrs. Gates too closely. She had the idea she had never seen anyone so perfectly presented.

"Do you want to set people on their heels? Your height should be an advantage."

Cassia smiled. "I have never found it so, but I've never been much interested in fashions."

"So, you only want my advice on gowns?"

"And accessories," Nora said, finding her voice. "I want my stepdaughter to look as lovely as she is."

"That's quite a compliment." A pleasant smile curled the corners of Mrs. Gates' mouth.

Cassia shrugged. "I have no taste. I have interests other than dressing."

"Nevertheless, I can give you a style that will impress, should you offer me the task." Mrs. Gates sat, her hands clasped, awaiting an answer.

Cassia wouldn't have been human not to envy Mrs. Gates her looks. The widow had large eyes, a small straight nose and perfect posture. Although she wore the usual stays, her body, even her hands had a natural shapeliness. A man would want to hold this loveliness in his arms. She would not remain a widow for too long. Cassia doubted she could impart her natural beauty to any of her protégées but if she could impart her dress sense, Cassia would be delighted.

The woman dressed simply with neither patterns nor frills. The gray of her round gown toned down the natural warmth of her skin. When Cassia wore gray, she depressed herself. "I would like to offer you the task," she said, smiling. "I have never found a color that suits me."

"You want warm colors with your light skin and hair, though I suspect a very dark shade of cool colors would suit you as well. We can experiment until we find the exact shades for you. Many women would kill to have your pale blonde hair."

"They wouldn't kill to have my pale eyelashes."

Mrs. Gates offered a thinking smile. "Easily fixed with

blacking. Shall we start tomorrow? If you leave your address with me, I will call on you in the morning. Shall we say ten?"

Nora rose. "We shall say ten."

Subsequently, at ten the next morning, Nora ushered Mrs. Gates into Cassia's bedroom. "I'll leave you to it. Your father wishes to visit the maritime exhibition. He honestly thinks I would enjoy it, too. I can't imagine why, when I could discuss gowns instead and play with baby Jack." Her expression distracted, she left.

Staring after her, Cassia said, "Good morning, Mrs. Gates. I thought I ought to save time and look over my gowns." She removed her plain pink gown from the shelves. "I wasn't sure if we could add another trimming to change this."

"Perhaps." Mrs. Gates glanced over the frilly blue gown Cassia wore. "I think the removal of the train on this one will make quite a difference. And you could lower the neckline so that the blue is not so close to your face."

"Would that help?"

"A trimming in another color would help, too."

"What other color?"

Mrs. Gates smiled. "A warmer color. A light green, perhaps patterned. The pink on the bed should be quite simple to update. Are you a skilled sewer?"

"Adequate, when forced. What do you suggest?"

"Again, change the neckline. The ladies are exposing quite a lot of bosom this year. But, pink is pretty on you. It only wants a little updating. The darker blue …"

"Donate it to a charity?"

Mrs. Gates laughed. "Not at all. I don't see a problem in

you wearing the darker colors but if you want a renewal, you could put a floral edge around the neckline and the sleeves. Perhaps, we could choose a few contrasting fabrics today."

"Do you have a draper in mind?"

"We have a many such shops in London, Miss Lacey."

"I haven't explored any yet. I've toured the Tate and I've been to the museum."

"You've done your duty." Mrs. Gates showed two rounded cheeks when she smiled. "You ought to be enjoying yourself at your age."

"I enjoy myself by keeping busy at home. I wasn't cut out for balls and talking about other people."

"When you're married to the duke, you'll be living in a new social circle, one I know little about. However, I do know about the ball season. Everyone is busy socializing and meeting new contacts. All the young ladies are in the same position as you."

"They know each other. I'm new to them."

"Yesterday at the cricket match, I saw how comfortably you fit in. The Gerard girls seem quite smitten with you. I don't doubt that everyone else is too. You have a lovely smile and a friendly way. I think most of us envy you." Mrs. Gates held Cassia's gaze.

Cassia stared at the floor for a moment. "That's nice to hear. Thank you, Mrs. Gates. My stepmother will want to come with us to the dress shops."

"I'll wait for you both in the drawing room downstairs, in that case."

"How did you get here? Did you hire a carriage?"

"I have one at my disposal. The driver is waiting outside

to take us all wherever we wish to go." Mrs. Gates folded the blue bodice.

Cassia quickly donned her beige poke bonnet and her dark brown pelisse. Having a carriage at one's disposal seemed such a luxury. The old carriage they had been using had quite shocking springs and the seats had splits in the upholstery.

Knowing Nora would be downstairs, she strode with Mrs. Gates into the drawing room. Her father stood beside his wife, an expression of hope on his face. "Cassia, do you mind if we leave Mrs. Gates to take you out? Nora would like to see the exhibition with me."

"Go ahead. Enjoy yourselves. I'm sure we can manage without Nora." Cassia glanced at her stepmother who pulled down the corners of her mouth as if miserable. So much for wanting to see the exhibition. Cassie offered her a sympathetic smile.

Nora leaned forward and kissed Cassia on the cheek. "Take care of her, Mrs. Gates. She's our treasure."

Mrs. Gates didn't appear to be phased to have Cassia's charge. She escorted her to a shiny burgundy barouche with a smartly uniformed driver, who tipped his hat at Cassia. "This is more like it," she muttered not quite under her breath.

"The barouche? I only have it for a short time, but it's a luxury I certainly appreciate."

Cassia couldn't question her, but she mulled over the reason why a person might have a barouche on loan for a short time, and didn't come up with anything more suspicious than Mrs. Gates knowing someone who had no need of the vehicle. "We are using hired transport while we are in town. We had to hire a carriage to bring us to London, since we didn't have stabling. I suppose you would call us very countrified." Cassia settled into a seat upholstered in tan leather behind a driver who sat without slouching, ready to move off.

Mrs. Gates arranged her dark blue pelisse neatly as the horses responded to the flick of the reins. "I don't object to simplifying life. I wouldn't normally have transport either. I only have this because of the kindness of a friend. I'm not about to become accustomed to the luxury though I have it firmly in my mind that I would like to marry again and have something like this of my own."

"You must have liked being married the first time to be interested in having a second time."

"Women have little other choice, but I did like it the first time. I was very much in love with my husband."

Cassia briefly touched the other's woman's hand in sympathy. "Do you have any family in London?"

"Not a one. If I don't marry again, I can find work I enjoy, like this, playing with fabrics and styles."

"Better you than me. I would rather be working in my garden, or bothering the cook about meals."

"I'm sure being the wife of a duke will keep you busy." Mrs. Gates stared straight ahead.

Noting the bustle of the city, Cassia glanced at the rows of shops, most very smart. People seemed to have plenty to do, walking hither and thither, unlike she, who only had shopping to do. "I'm not trying for perfection and I do hope to be happy, of course." With the conversation heading in a direction she didn't mean to go, she smiled firmly, clutched her reticule, and waited for the carriage to pull up outside a row of small shops. Stepping out, she steeled herself.

Mrs. Gates stepped out behind her. "I can give you advice, but I won't tell you what to do."

Cassia didn't need advice to know that she looked like a French doll in her beige pelisse and she didn't mind at all. Or, not too much. "I know I'm sadly behind the new fashions but it didn't matter to me. And now I'm no longer on the market and I'll not need to go gallivanting."

"You may find your new husband is quite a man about town."

"Does that mean he will expect me to go about town with him?"

Mrs. Gates laughed. "He will expect you to be his hostess in the very least. I'm sure he would like to begin entertaining at home."

"Begin? Doesn't he entertain at home now?"

Mrs. Gates colored. "By all accounts he entertains at his club." Then she headed toward the single-fronted shop with Gordon's' Gowns painted in pink on the window. The doorbell tinkled as she headed inside.

Cassia hesitated a moment longer to examine the dress hanging from a stand in the centre front of the window. Then she followed. A woman wearing an utterly plain blue, beautifully cut gown, smiled and hurried over with a questioning smile on her face.

"Mrs. Gordon, may I introduce Miss Lacey to you? She is about to marry the Duke of Huntsdale." Mrs. Gates stepped back.

The woman, short and a little stout, with a happy face, angled her head slightly to the side and offered an impressed smile. "I would be most honored to make a gown for a prospective duchess. Do you know what you want?"

Mrs. Gates smiled. "Miss Lacey, did you see the gown in the window? I think it might look perfect on you."

Mrs. Gordon stared from the gown to Cassia and nodded. "It *would* flatter Miss Lacey's coloring."

"This is exactly the sort of advice I need, Mrs. Gates. I have no idea of fashion. Now, Mrs. Gordon, I *do* want to order gowns, but first I need one for my wedding, which is in two weeks. I'll have to have something finished by then." Cassia held her breath.

Mrs. Gordon pursed her lips. "If we can choose a fabric today, I should be able to have a gown ready for a fitting by the end of the week. Perhaps I should show you our white lace fabrics."

Cassia shook her head. "Please don't. I'm sure the duke would be delirious with joy if I wore anything else. I know lace is fashionable but he makes jokes about me in white lace. Mrs. Gates is here to help me with the color and fabric. As for other gowns, we could make a start today, but I won't need a thing until after the honeymoon."

Mrs. Gordon inclined her head. "What color are you planning to wear for your wedding?"

"Shall we look at everything, Mrs. Gates?" Cassia practically dusted off her gloves and led the way to the fabric room at the back of the shop.

On Tuesday, three days before her wedding, Cassia stood in the fitting room of Gordon's Gowns staring critically at the pale green silk gown she planned to wear for her wedding. Mrs. Gates had decided that an elaborately puffed orange trimming should be added around the lowered neckline and on the tiny sleeves. After the wedding, Cassia would wear this with a delicious green bonnet decorated with darker green leaves. The ensemble was the most sophisticated outfit she had ever worn.

Until Mrs. Gates had suggested the color, Cassia had never thought to wear such an interesting green but the gold tint in the trimming highlighted the blue of her eyes. Her pinkish skin also looked fresher and cooler. "I don't want to admire myself, because it's the gown that looks elegant rather than I." She swished the skirts and inspected herself from every angle, pleased by her appearance for the first time in her life.

"You look very lovely, Miss Lacey," Mrs. Gordon said from behind Mrs. Gates, but she would say that because she was selling Cassia a very expensive gown. Cassia waited for a comment from Mrs. Gates whose taste she much admired.

"She is right, Miss Lacey." Mrs. Gates nodded. "The colors you wore previously, the pinks and the blues, were a little insipid for your coloring. We can now see *you* rather than the gowns you wear. This one is plain enough to set off your looks. Have you finished the alterations on Miss Lacey's white lace evening gown, Mrs. Gordon? We could take both today if you wish."

"Miss Lacey might like to try on the garment on first." Mrs. Gordon left for a moment and returned with her lacy skirts topped by a puffy-sleeved dropped-shoulder bodice in a darkish teal, trimmed with tiny white lace roses around the neckline. This also looked far more sophisticated than Cassia had expected. Fussy details, clearly, were not for her. The bodice fitted perfectly and Mrs. Gordon packed everything into a box lined with tissue paper.

"I doubt the green gown will be particularly happy with my red velvet shoes," Cassia said in a hinting voice.

The tiny dimple appeared in Mrs. Gates' cheek. "I think the gown would scream for mercy at the sight."

"So, we should buy evening shoes, too," Cassia said firmly, stepping back into her blue gown. "What color?"

"Any color. Any fabric. You would need to have them made I expect, but shall we try the shoemaker?"

"Yes, indeed." Cassia waited to be hooked up, and then she snuggled into her beige pelisse and placed her bonnet carefully, making a bow of the new burgundy ribbons. Turning, she tucked her hand beneath Mrs. Gates' elbow. "Do you have a first name, Mrs. Gates?"

The other woman looked surprised, but pleased. "I believe so." She smiled. "Amelia. Please make use of it."

"I would be delighted. The full name or Mellie?"

"I prefer to be called Amelia."

"It's a lovely name. My name is Cassiopeia but everyone calls me Cassia."

"Cassia and Amelia it is." Still smiling, Amelia walked outside with Cassia attached. She spoke to the barouche driver who moved off without them.

Cassia had been confined to the house for far too long. Happy in the outdoors, she marched off down the busy thoroughfare where other shoppers moved along glancing in shop windows or entering premises intending to buy the best bargains, much needed goods, or anything at all sold in the street. The old buildings loomed high, and carriages passed full of shoppers or spectators.

During a delightfully gossipy hour with the interesting woman who had the fashion style that she lacked, Cassia chose two ridiculously adorable hats, one fashionably embellished with bunches of colorful flowers. She also found self-patterned white shoes, leaving an order for the same style in green.

Finally, loaded with her parcels, at the designated time, she and Amelia stepped into the barouche that had miraculously appeared in the front of the dress shop. After a clipping pace through the streets, the driver drew up to the door of her father's hired house. "Stay and have tea with me, Amelia." Cassia rested her hand on the other lady's forearm. "I want to show you the changes to the rest of my wardrobe. Unless you have a line of clients awaiting you?"

"I don't. Not a single one. Tea would be very welcome." Amelia closed her parasol and stepped out of the carriage behind Cassia. She lowered her voice as she followed Cassia to the front door. "I feel so guilty with all this stopping and starting and leaving the driver to wait. He says it's his job and he is just as happy to idle as to drive, but I wonder what the horses think?"

"If they're anything like our horses, they change their minds from minute to minute, but I've yet to see an idling horse anxious to get back to work. See? They're happy with a bag of chaff, and I won't keep you forever."

"And I won't keep the *carriage* forever." Amelia sighed. "Having transport is a luxury but rather awkward for a city dweller with no stabling. My friend meant to be kind, but I find it easier to walk or call for a hackney."

Cassia pushed the front door open. "I'll just stop by the kitchen and order tea in the sitting room."

Amelia awaited her at the bottom of the stairs and together with the parcels they trudged up, Amelia looking as pleased as Cassia.

Together they carefully laid out the wedding gown and the new bodice on the bed. Cassia dragged her pale blue skirt out of the chest. "I want you to see what the new trimming looks like. Did I make the right choices?"

"The green stripe on the blue looks very nice. And this floral on the pink certainly helps to break up the color."

"You're congratulating yourself, you know. I'm only the person who did the sewing."

"You sew beautifully, far better than I can." Amelia smiled. "As for your white lace gown, you can change that any time you like with another under-gown, but perhaps you could lower the neckline. More skin would certainly help there. In any event, at least you have another option."

"We've expanded my wardrobe greatly by adding only one new bodice and a wedding gown. If I can find the time, I'll do as you advise with the lace gown."

"Mrs. Gordon will finish your other gowns while you are on your honeymoon."

Cassia carefully folded the new bodice. "My stepmother plans to leave for Surrey after she has seen us off. I will have to make morning calls alone, and I'm not looking forward to that."

"It never hurts to get to know people, Cassia."

Cassia sighed. "I'm sure a duchess will need to know more people than a country miss but I am sure I will have much to do in my new home."

Amelia's dimple appeared again. "And I'm sure your new husband will want to keep you there."

Cassia cleared her throat. She had wanted to discuss Huntsdale and what she should expect on her wedding night. The embarrassment factor stopped her from asking Nora or her father, who gave her the impression they thought she had already anticipated the event. "When I barely knew Huntsdale, he was supposed to be looking after me, finding me partners at a ball, which he did very well, until he took me into the supper room at the assembly rooms and kissed me."

Amelia lifted her eyebrows. "And didn't you like that?"

"Well ... he was supposed to be making the man I expected to marry jealous, so I should have been grateful. But at the time I was quite nervous. I don't want to look like a bumpkin on my wedding night."

A quick smile crossed Amelia's face. "He is a very attractive man, Cassia, and experienced. He will take care of you. Do you have a seductive nightgown?"

"No, and I don't plan to buy one. I'd rather wear something to put him off." Cassia folded her arms.

Amelia's eyes sparked with amusement. "If he wants you, you won't be able to put him off."

"Is that what men are like? Do they insist on their marital rights?"

"A wise man wouldn't. He would charm you so beautifully that you would insist on *your* marital rights."

"Amelia, you are a shocking woman. I knew you would be the one to ask." Cassia rarely giggled, but she couldn't stop herself. "So, it's not too uncomfortable?"

"Not if you are in the mood, and a wise husband would make sure you are in the mood."

"He would know how to do that because he had a mistress." Cassia firmed her mouth.

Amelia's face lost all expression. "It's not an unusual thing when young men have no recourse other than from women of the night who may have contracted nasty diseases."

"Really? I thought it was rather shocking."

Amelia drew a deep breath. "Abstinence is the only other choice. I fear few young men practice it. Oh, to be young and giddy again."

Without her dark hat, Amelia didn't look much past the first blush of youth, herself. She wore her soft curly auburn hair lightly gathered in an upsweep again. "Have you been widowed for a long time?"

"Three years. My husband died after four years of marriage."

"That must have been very difficult for you."

"I have a small annuity but that won't last forever. I thought I should try my only skill, social engineering."

Cassia laughed and led the way back down the stairs. "Social engineering? That sounds very important."

"I think so. It's better than being called a gown-trimmer or whatever I may be."

"You're a miracle worker. You're teaching me how to dress and that's no mean feat. My mother couldn't and Nora certainly can't. She is fond of pastels and frills herself." Cassia opened the door to the drawing room. A teapot, two cups, sugar, and milk sat on the side table. The grumpy cook had done well. "Next time you come to call,

I'll bake a cake. This cook only deals with the essentials, like meals. You will come to call after I am married, too, won't you?"

"I would be delighted, Cassia." Amelia dropped her gaze. "But I'm not sure that a woman in my position would be welcomed as friend for you by your husband."

Cassia poured the tea. Her father had taken note of her friends, but had never commented. As she accepted his friends, he accepted hers. Without a doubt, Huntsdale would have the same mindset. "I don't let anyone tell me who I may have as a friend."

Chapter Eight

On her wedding day, Cassia stood before the mirror in awed silence, while she inspected her appearance. With great courtesy, and possibly a touch of relief, Nora had left Cassia to the expert, Amelia, who understood the niceties of shoulder lines, the puff of sleeves, and the dressing of hair. She had also decided that Cassia's hair should be smoothed back from her face and taken straight to the crown of her head. Tiny plaits made a crisscross pattern around the bunch from which a few long curls spiraled.

"I'm not showing a scrap of maidenly modesty, am I, staring at myself like this?" She glanced at her friend who was reflected in the mirror behind her. "I am simply astounded by how interesting I look in these colors. I seem like someone else entirely."

"You look like the *you* that you were meant to be. I don't think you know how utterly lovely you are." Amelia's tawny eyes glowed with sincerity. She wore a dark pink gown that, with her hair color, could have included her in a Renaissance painting.

Not one to be overly emotional, Cassia put her hands on Amelia's shoulders and swooped a kiss onto each of her cheeks. "I couldn't have had anyone better to help me dress. Nora would have insisted I looked lovely and I wouldn't have believed her because if I had worn whatever she and I together might have chosen, I would have looked more like the spinster aunt than the bride." Cassia scanned herself again.

Somehow, Huntsdale, who tended to want to organize everything, had managed to persuade Mrs. Gordon to finish a going-away outfit for Cassia in a few days. She suspected an exorbitant amount of money had changed hands, but since in a day she would be married to the man with the money, she didn't quibble. For the first time in her life, she could have said, if she *had* discussed any payment, *spare no expense,* for clearly none had been spared.

"You don't have as little sense of style as you think."

"Or else I wouldn't know I don't have a sense of style." Because during the past week Cassia had spent a part of each day awkwardly trying to get to know Huntsdale, or Adam, as he has asked her to call him, she had missed being with her friend. "I've hardly seen you this week. I have done nothing for the past few days but indulge myself with social events and dressmakers. I think this is the first moment I've had to gossip."

Amelia smiled and shook her head. "I've had no time, either. I've had to get half a dozen young ladies fashionably dressed for your wedding. No one speaks about anything else."

"I know you need to hover around the new debutants, but I'm sure I won't be the only married lady who will need your services." Cassia turned her back to the mirror and examined her new shoes. She should have worn them in, but she'd not had the time. "Only the other day, Nora mentioned how much money you had saved us with your economical ideas."

"That's the problem, Cassia." Amelia settled the pleats at Cassia's high waistline. "You won't need to practice economy once you are married to the duke. Therefore, you won't need me."

"I'll still want you as a friend, though."

Amelia smiled wryly. "If I had an ounce of business sense, I would use your wedding as an advertisement for my economical ideas. *How to catch a duke with economical gowns.*"

Cassia laughed. "Strictly speaking, he has never mentioned my gowns other than to insult them. It should be *how to catch a wealthy duke by not trying to catch a wealthy duke.*" She blushed. "And I didn't. Try."

"You didn't need to. Anyone can see he is smitten. I only wish I had the same luck." Amelia's smile was rueful.

Cassia glanced away. Although she would have liked to tell Amelia the true story of Adam's proposal, that he had asked for her hand because he was a gentleman, she had given her father her promise to remain discreet. "I don't doubt some smart man will fall desperately in love with you."

Amelia heaved a breath. "The only man for me doesn't see me as the only woman for him."

"In that case, we must stay in this room until you tell me all about this strange creature."

Amelia shook her head, smiling. "Today is your last day of freedom. That is certainly a cause for celebration. As for men, pah! All the unavailable must be forgotten forthwith."

"Yes, pah! My only other prospect let me down badly. He arrived back in town yesterday. And none too soon, I told him, if he wanted to carry me off before I married one of his friends."

Amelia's expression stilled. "You're not serious?"

Cassia laughed. "About George? Of course not. After meeting Adam, I see I could never have married George. Anyway, George told me that his father has decided his time as a carefree bachelor is at an end. He has given him employment and now he will be living in town permanently. He is supposed to be managing his father's shipping interests."

"I suppose that will mean spending time at the docks supervising the loading and unloading?" Amelia asked, noticing a lose thread on Cassia's glove and snapping it off.

"I think he'll mainly be giving his opinions to other people. He told me I'll do well with Adam. Dreadful man. What would he know?"

"Supposedly he knows the duke and approves of him as a husband."

"It's not for him to approve or disapprove, but I'm glad that he has decided to do something with his life." Cassia picked up the choker of pearls and peridots that Huntsdale had sent over with matching earrings for her to wear on this day of days. "I'm extremely lucky, Amelia. The two people I like most in the world are now living in town with me."

Amelia fastened the clip for her. The stones matched

Cassia's gown and had formerly belonged to Adam's mother. Now Cassia's, the set could not be recognized as being borrowed. She would have to classify the necklace as something old. Suddenly sentimental, she caught Amelia's gaze. "May I borrow a handkerchief from you? It occurs to me that I have nothing borrowed to wear for my wedding."

"Of course you may." Amelia's eyes glossed slightly. "I do hope I never disappoint you, Cassia."

"I hope I never disappoint you, either."

She kept that thought in her head while standing at the altar of St. Luke's church, staring at the stained glass window while the minister droned on about nothing she could absorb. Behind her sat almost the entire population of London, staring at the pleats in the back of her gown, wondering how on earth the most eligible male in England came to be marrying a rigid, terrified country woman.

Adam decided that the wedding went rather well. After the breakfast, his guests followed him outside the hall Cedric had chosen for the reception, deeming the town house unsuitable, to watch his travelling carriage pull up at the front, awaiting him and his new bride. Cassia's boxes and cases had been strapped onto the back during the wedding ceremony. Behind him stood the whole of London's society.

During the ceremony, people he barely knew had filled the church, and the overflow stood outside. Only the top fifty on his list of acquaintances had been invited to the breakfast. He needed daylight for the long drive into Kent where he planned to spend his week-long honeymoon. Cedric had assured him he could spare the time.

Cassia looked surprisingly beautiful. Amelia, although lacking respectability, certainly had taste. She had made sure Cassia wore a gown for the ceremony that suited her curved body and accented the ice blue of her eyes. Her hair had always been wondrous, the color unlike that of anyone else, almost silver blonde, worn in a soft arrangement at the top of her head. She had accepted the necklace he'd had delivered to her house this morning, his mother's triple row of pearls. Diamonds would have been inappropriate to wear in the morning, he knew that, but awaiting her when they arrived back in town was his wedding present to her, a long rope of the finest stones set in gold.

Planning to arrive at his country estate during the late afternoon, he handed her into the carriage. She wore a simpler gown for travelling, a plain tangerine with pleating on the bodice, and warm brown pelisse. Another carriage would follow behind transporting his valet and two footmen. He kept only a skeleton staff at Huntsdale House, a team of gardeners, a housekeeper, a cook, a butler, and a few housemaids. He rarely invited guests. The butler would make sure the house would be ready to receive the new mistress. He hoped the new mistress was ready to receive the master. For two weeks he had thought of nothing other than her beautiful body, which he planned to disrobe inch by inch, kiss by kiss.

"You may be surprised to hear this, but I have never been to Kent." Cassia began fussing with her skirts on the seat.

He waited for her to settle and then he sat beside her. "I imagine you had no reason."

"Not when I lived in the most beautiful part of this country for the whole of my life." She said this with her chin raised, as if parts of the country needed to compete.

"I'm hoping you will think my part is equally good." The innuendo sounded appalling. He avoided her gaze.

Apparently her mind didn't focus on incidentals like his impressionable body. "I believe most people grow apples and pears in Kent. Perhaps that will remind me of home." Blinking hard, she stared out the window as they pulled onto the carriageway.

He tried again. "The wedding went well."

"Your Mr. Rogers is extremely efficient."

"You don't need to be nervous, Cassia. Nothing will happen to you without your permission."

"So I had surmised. You have been incredibly trustworthy to date. But you must remember that we barely know each other."

He left that one alone. The moment he had met her, he had wanted to upend her, which was the reason why he had paid off Mellie. No one would do for him but Cassia of the mischievous eyes, the dry sense of humor, and the beautiful healthy body. He wanted her with an ache that suffused his entire being.

And tonight, God willing, he would finally have her.

During the journey through the undulating hills, Cassia learned her new husband wasn't a plausible charmer like

George. Adam spoke in short, fact-filled sentences. He focused more on realities than trivialities. She couldn't imagine him ever exploring the feelings of others or arguing about the nuances in a line of poetry. He enjoyed numbers. Despite his shortcomings, he made the journey interesting by pointing out various aspects of the scenery.

By the time they arrived in his part of Kent, she had her bearings, and as they drove past, duly noted great height of the uneven hedges that hid the Gerard's country house from public view. Reaching Adam's property took the carriage farther along the same narrow road, finally turning down a long drive guarded by tall poplars. An Elizabethan edifice appeared, as if growing out of the smooth winter green fields. The carriages stopped near to the red brick entrance of a house that loomed four stories high.

Adam waited for the coachman to tie the weary horses and let down the steps. Once on his own soil, he brushed down his jacket, and offered his hand to Cassia. She scrambled out on unsteady legs, hoping she didn't appear awkward, for a man and a woman stood outside the front door, smiling a welcome. Adam greeted both and turned to Cassia. "My new duchess, may I present Mrs. Giddings, the housekeeper, and Mr. Hodges, the butler."

The housekeeper curtsied as if Cassia might be royalty and the butler bowed. Formalities over, the luggage was taken into the house by a burly footman. Adam's valet trotted behind with his dressing case. Cassia followed her husband into a massive drafty hall.

"You could hold a ball in this space," she said staring at high ceilings. "It is enormous."

"My parents did quite a bit of entertaining here, mainly

country house parties. We have more than twenty bedrooms, but that part of the house hasn't been open since my parents died. I've never found the time, or even the need. Perhaps you will change that."

Cassia couldn't see herself as a society matron, but she honestly enjoyed having guests, always had. She offered him a weak smile. "Though, perhaps not this week. What's this room?" She indicated the enormous doorway to the immediate left.

"The formal reception area. The room farther along is the library. The room on the right is now a withdrawing room. The passage here leads down to the kitchens and the servant's quarters."

At that moment, the carriage moved off to the coach house and the second took the place at the front. Two tall footmen leapt out, their voices carrying until they spotted Cassia glancing at them through the open front door. Immediately they each grabbed up a portmanteau and hurried into the house. Apparently they knew their way around. They scurried off toward the kitchens.

"I'll show you upstairs to the bedroom wing." Adam indicated the grand staircase that curved in a semicircle so that the top ended up facing the front of the house.

She followed him. "I would be interested in the amenities," she mentioned awkwardly.

"The bathrooms? We have quite a few. My father modernized some years ago. Ours is up here on the other side of the landing. This is where we will sleep." He opened the door to a bedroom the size of a drawing room, oppressively decorated in red velvet. "But I see you are more interested in refreshing yourself." His eyes gleamed with amusement.

She edged back toward the bathroom, assuming rightly that a man as wealthy as his father would have installed a water closet. The room contained a large window. The view of the garden was extensive from up here. The near view had been planted with a selection of camellias and smaller shrubs. The aspect at the side showed a walled vegetable garden and rows of fruit trees. Instantly, she relaxed. While here, she could spend time in the garden, repairing her fractured soul. Never had she expected to be married in haste, or in front of so many people who attended her wedding merely to speculate on the reason for such haste.

She returned to her bedroom to find one of the maids unpacking for her in the adjoining dressing room. Adam had disappeared. Soon she would need to change for dinner. She had barely untied the ribbons on her hat as the housekeeper knocked and entered. "The cook asked if you would inspect the meal for tonight, if it is not too much trouble for your grace."

"Certainly. I'll come straight away." She left her hat and pelisse on the bed.

Mrs. Giddings took her a flight below the reception rooms, where the aroma of roasting meat wafted through the side passage that led to a vast area with a wood stove set into the far wall. The glow of the sunset glinted on the cook's spoon, which he held upright while scanning a recipe book opened on the central work area. He raised his head, directing his wary gaze at Cassia. "I know ze duke likes good plain food and I'm preparing roast pigeons wiz a rabbit ragout. Will zat do?"

Cassia had no idea of Adam's tastes. "Perhaps a few vegetable dishes too," she said firmly. "As well as fruit and cheese." She sighed. The kitchen was a mess. The peelings still sat in the table. The cook didn't appear to be a man who had any idea of how to organize and if he had an assistant, he or she was invisible. Disaster seemed imminent. "Should I help?"

"Ze duke he would have my head if I let his duchess help."

"I don't expect he will know. Where are the maids?" She glanced at Mrs. Giddings.

"Floss is dusting the upstairs rooms, your grace, and Elsie is getting the dining room ready."

"Only two? Send them to me." Cassia swung out of the kitchen.

Her husband, the duke, deserved payment in kind for his efforts. He had wed a woman he thought might make him comfortable, and had paid for and organized a huge wedding and a breakfast. After having made a speech or two, and then being pummeled by a long journey, tonight he would at least have a good meal in a well-ordered house.

Mrs. Giddings was not capable of giving him either. Cassia could do both.

After wandering around the moisture-laden gardens for more than an hour, leaving Cassia to discover what she would inside, Adam dressed for dinner and presented himself in the sitting room. Cassia had changed into an evening gown with a white lace skirt and a dark blue bodice.

She still wore the peridot choker, which didn't look quite right with her outfit. Perhaps she had no other jewelry. He would soon fix that. She could have anything she wanted.

"Thank you for today," she said in a polite voice. She patted the front of her skirts before she sat. "You made the whole charade so easy. When we get back to town, what shall I do other than listen to the effuse compliments I will now receive after being so clever as to have landed a rich duke?"

His shoulders relaxed. "First, I plan to show you off everywhere I can. My secretary has orders to accept every invitation I have received for the next month. Naturally, we shall take this week for ourselves."

She gave a hesitant smile. "I expect I shall have many duties to perform. I hope to be of use to you as your hostess, which is a job I enjoy very much. I'm also very fond of gardens, as I have told you. Do you have a nice one in your city house?"

"My mother planted a very fine garden there. I hope you will like it. You may not have noticed, but I also have a large garden here."

"I will look forward to exploring."

"As will I, Cassia."

She stiffened her spine, answering with a cynical smile that revealed her suspicions. "Surely you have seen your garden before."

"I wasn't referring to my garden ... as you rightly surmised." He paused, blinking with concentration. "I am a wealthy man whose role in life is to maintain various land holdings with which to support my extended family and dependents. You could describe me as a businessman. I pay a personal secretary, and I have a full staff in most of my houses, but having the support of a wife would ease my load considerably. Any amount of women could fit my specifications." His shoulders lifted, involuntarily. "But I want you, Cassia."

She blinked. "You hardly know me. If not for that wretched locked door, you could have had anyone else."

He stared at her, his mood darkening. "Had? You mean I could *buy*, don't you?" Of course, when he wanted a woman, he could always buy a new mistress, but mistresses and wives were not to be confused. No man with any pride would stoop to purchasing a wife. He had, instead, found an obstinate and strong-minded woman whose body he wanted as much as her mind, and he had managed to marry her with a little help from his graceless friends, which was certainly not the same thing.

She offered a non-committal shrug. "Although your money is no doubt attractive to women, you know very well that you are tall and handsome. If you are angling for a compliment, don't expect one from woman who hadn't considered marriage to you."

He blew out a breath. At least, she had complimented him. His shoulders relaxed. After assiduously courting her for the past three weeks and receiving no more than a wary friendship for his efforts, he would accept any encouragement. Friendship was, of course, not enough for him. He wanted the marriage his parents hadn't managed, one comprising mutual respect. If Cassia learned to care for him, he would be well satisfied.

Having had his bedroom manners taught to him by Mellie, he knew the art of seduction. Taking a step forward, he took Cassia's hands, clasping each, palm against palm, fingers entwined. Her gaze lifted to his. While he focused on her mouth, he slowly moved her hands behind her while she watched his face. Held against his pounding heart, she accepted his lips touching hers. Because he wanted her willing, he let her hands go and found that she meant to do nothing more than rest her hands on his chest. He settled his on the small of her back.

She seemed to breathe him in. Her kiss was somewhat akin to the response she had given him at the supper dance but far more restrained. Despite the layers of fabric between them, his body expressed his blatant interest. He eased back, not wanting to rush her.

Her breath warmed his neck, but since she had moved her hands to the front of his chest, he began another kiss on her lips. While absorbed in teasing his mouth lightly against hers, his mind wandered to the bedroom and the night ahead. A rush of desire shortened his breath. And then the butler oozed into the room and announced dinner. Cassia pushed herself out of his arms, and turned.

Trying to ignore the thudding of his heart, he walked behind her. The dining room looked a little different tonight, shinier, smarter. The formal table had a least two leaves removed. He seated Cassia, and sat at the head, noting that his old monogrammed napkin ring marked his place. The two foot high epergne had been moved to the sideboard. "This is novel," he said, inclining his head in the direction of the monstrosity. "We'll be able to see each other. My mother didn't want to see my father."

She smiled. "I've only been married a day. Perhaps next week I will want the epergne put back."

He smiled firmly. By next week, she would be pliant in his arms. "Did your visit to the kitchen go well?"

"You will know when you taste the food. I've never seen anything quite as amusing as watching Elsie peel vegetables. She managed the job like a princess born, with her arms outstretched and her nose wrinkled in distaste. I asked her if she would like me to take over the peeling while she cleaned the sinks. Her arm distance shrank immediately."

Startled, he stiffened. "It's not your place to peel vegetables."

"No need to look so haughty. As a job, it's not unpleasant. I fear your servants have been spoiled with no one but you and your brother to tend."

"That could be so," he said slowly. "In town, we entertain at our club and we often eat there too. We only keep a skeletal staff, here."

"I hope you don't mind if I change those arrangements once we return home."

A place inside him warmed when she said *home*. He hoped she would adjust as quickly as she indicated she was prepared to do. "You are the mistress. You must run our houses the way you see fit."

"In that case, I'll need to spend more time in the kitchen. Your cook is no cook."

"He has always done the cooking here."

"Since you rarely stay here, it may not matter, but I hope I will spend more time here and less in London, in which case, I would prefer someone who doesn't need my supervision. I hope you don't mind that I have changed the way a few tasks are done, already. I don't see the point of using preserves if you have fresh fruit available. You have a vegetable garden and an orchard. Mr. Giddings found fresh greens, and the yard boy picked the ripe fruit in the orchard. What did you do while I was prodding your servants into action?"

"I explored the garden." He smiled. "Not that I particularly wanted to, but the head gardener told me a few weeks ago that a few trees needed removing, and he wants decisions on plantings. I know nothing about the garden and have no particular interest as long as the place is tidy. So, I pottered around, keeping out of his sight."

"If that is how much you enjoy country life, your honeymoon here will bore you."

"I don't think so."

He knew she understood the reference when she blushed.

Cassia decided the dinner went over rather well. The custard was light and the stewed plums sufficiently tart to balance the sweetness. Elsie remembered to serve from the right and remove from the left. Cassia suspected she would need to teach all the parlor maids in town the same. Or did Adam have footmen to wait at the tables? She knew nothing about him, and had never seen the house she would be occupying as his wife, but, the more problems, the better. She would be tremendously bored living in the city without having an enormous garden to tend.

Clearly, she was expected to amuse herself in the sitting room after dinner while Adam occupied his study. Although she wasn't keen on embroidery, she might have to take up the occupation if he continued leaving her to her own devices. If the man wanted a pleasant relationship in the bedroom at night, he would do well to continue charming her during the day. The light faded while she read a book she found in the dusty library. Finally, she lit a lamp. He appeared in the doorway. "The servants wish to retire for the night. They begin work early. Would you like to retire now or should I keep you company?"

"I don't see the harm in talking to each other."

He sat in the armchair adjacent to her. "Your book is dull?"

"Not at all. I've always been interested in the parasites found in the southern regions of India."

He laughed. "Would you like a glass of brandy?"

She nodded, willing to try anything to ease the nervousness caused by the night ahead.

He rose and rang for the butler, who brought back two enormous balloon glasses and bottle. "This brandy should be well-aged. I haven't touched a drop of this in years." Huntsdale poured an inch or two into each and brought both over.

A single sniff of hers and her eyes watered, but she took a sip. Heat travelled down her throat and into her chest. Although she didn't like the taste, the spreading warmth helped to relax her. "I'm nervous, you know." Her voice seemed to echo out of the glass.

"About sharing a bed?"

"Of course."

"Nothing will happen that you don't want to happen."

"But it has to happen eventually."

"We want children, don't we?"

She nodded.

"My thought is that the sooner we start becoming accustomed to each other, the better. If you don't like anything I do, you only need to tell me to stop." Sitting on the edge of his chair, he stared at the glass he held between his knees. Yet again, the thickness of his eyelashes took her by surprise.

She managed another large gulp and noticed he barely took a sip. If one of them needed to be soused, better she than he. She breathed out the fumes and took in more brandy. The next time she spared him a glance, she found she had a smile on her face. If she giggled she would hate herself but the tickle inside that had caused the smile seemed likely to follow through with a laugh. Pressing her lips together, she concentrated his sheer, overwhelming lack of charm. He relied on his physicality and his money get by. A man like him would surely be dependable.

"I think I am ready to go upstairs."

Chapter Nine

Knowing that the main bedroom only had a single dressing room, entered from the hallway, Cassia pondered the arrangements. "Will you use the dressing room, first?" she asked, hesitating at the door.

Adam half smiled and indicated that she could enter. He followed her into a large space lined with drawers and shelves. She turned to face him, He had removed his coat and had begun untying the complicated knot of his cravat. He didn't glance at her.

"I think I should wait in the bedroom until you have finished."

"I'm sure you noticed that I have dismissed the servants for the night. If you want help with your lacing, I'm the only person who can help you."

"I won't need help, thank you."

"May the Lord have mercy on you, if I finish undressing and you call me back in here to undo anything." His gaze met and held hers. "We managed in the shed and that was a space very much smaller than this," he said, pulling his shirt out of his breeches.

"We weren't undressing."

He stopped and glanced at her. "I distinctly recall needing to remove my jacket and cravat."

She cast a narrow eyed glance at him. Before dinner, Elsie had helped her dress. Although Cassia could manage on her own, and had many times, she heeded his warning. Nothing would be more embarrassing than to have to ask him to come back and help her. Without another word, she stepped out of shoes and made sure her dressing robe was within reaching distance. Then she turned her back on him and discreetly pulled off her stockings. Her stays had laces, which she had no inclination to try to undo while he watched.

The flutter of her pulse embarrassing her, she dropped her hands to her sides and flexed her fingers, ready to start contorting herself.

He moved in front of her, his chest bare. Not quite bare. Just unclothed. A tee shape of dark hair covered some of his skin. She averted her gaze, her cheeks a little warm, her heart thumping. Although she couldn't say she was intimidated, she could admit to being nervous.

"Let me help," he said, tossing his shirt in the corner. "I think I can manage your stays for you."

"I'm happy to manage on my own, thank you."

He made an incredulous face, turned her, and began at the top, while her stiff finders flexed. His breath stirred the hair on her nape. After finishing with her laces, he placed a kiss at the juncture of her neck and shoulders. She shivered, turning her head and glancing over her shoulder at him, trying to read his expression, but the man had largely been a mystery to her. She had no idea why he hadn't objected to marrying her. After all, a man with his money could have anyone.

As hastily as she could manage, she shimmied out of her gown. Her chemise protected her modesty. Although she ought to be a blushing bride, the night ahead held no true terrors for a country-woman. Like any other, she had a reasonable idea of what would happen. Her only worry was the awkwardness of the situation. She barely knew her husband, not that she thought having marital relations with any man she did know would be any less awkward, but she had promised herself in marriage and she expected to produce a clutch of children. Maidenly modesty had no place in her life. She would spend many years with this large and uncompromising man, and she may as well start as she meant to go on—with confidence.

Although her curiosity niggled at her, she couldn't watch him undress himself, while she needed to slip into her night attire without exposing her entire body. She managed this one arm at a time. When she finally faced him fully covered in her white cotton nightgown, he had donned a black silk banyan. She hoped she hid her breathless admiration. Nothing could have looked more perfect with his dark hair and light eyes.

With a courteous smile on his face, he ushered her out of the dressing room and into the bedroom. "Do you have a preferred side to sleep?" he asked, staring at the enormous old-fashioned four-poster bed.

Fortunately, the bed could fit another two people. "I expect you would rather be closer to the door. The window side will suit me." Her chest full of skittering butterflies, she walked to that side, bumping her knee on the corner post. While her back had been turned, he apparently removed his robe and slid between the sheets. His muscular chest was exposed as he leaned back against the carved headboard, his arms folded behind his head. If the rest of him was also naked, well, she couldn't quite reveal the rest of herself to him at this stage. Letting him see her undress was unsettling enough for the first night.

Grabbing a breath, she slipped into the bed beside him. Fortunately, the night was mild and the sheets had been warmed. At first, she lay on her back, wondering how matters would proceed. She clasped her fingers together and risked a glance at him. He elevated his eyebrows, not quite smiling, turned away, and smothered the lamp wick. Now, she lay with him in the dark. Although she had spent a dark night with him before, the back of her neck ached with tension.

Meanwhile, his movements indicated that he had moved down in the bed. She copied him, lying flat on her back, wishing she knew what he intended to do. Suddenly, his dark shadow loomed over her in the dark. Her body reacted by stiffening.

"Cassia," he said in a husky whisper. His body radiated heat. He placed a soft kiss onto the base of her throat, leaving a tingle that reached her lower abdomen.

Suddenly she couldn't breathe. Overwhelmed by panic, she slid her elbows between them, flattening her palms on the hard wall of his chest, ready to push him away if need be, but he gently tucked her into him. In a trice, she lay hard up against a hard torso, hot and bothered, and so nervous that she couldn't even swallow. His hand rucked up her nightgown, and landed on the skin of her back, large and warm. Her body tensed, but she knew that the sooner her deflowering was over and done with, the better.

He pressed his lips gently over the sensitive area below her ear. Her heart began to skip beats, fully conscious that she lay clasped against a naked man. Breathing in and out, she slowly calmed herself enough to realize that the naked man appeared to be taking his time. He held her, tasting her skin, not attempting to do more. She tried her best to relax, easing her shoulders, and giving in to the urge to touch the rasp of his shaven jaw. The sensuous texture shot a thrill throughout her entire body.

His head tilted and he mouthed the skin between her thumb and forefinger, while shifting slightly to move her hand behind his head. Her body fully against his, she began to breathe through her mouth, noting his every movement. The knowledge that she would live with this large, commanding man for the rest of her life, running his home and having his children, almost overwhelmed her.

When his male body part began to nudge into her belly, she clung far too tightly to him. Certain that he would be expecting her to act like a modest young virgin, she stayed as still as a statue. Then his lips covered hers. He began to spread gentle kisses all over her face, using a soft, careful mouth. Her skin heated. With no idea how to respond, she curled her fingers around his biceps. His whole body was hard and muscular, causing her to wonder yet again what he saw in her. She ached and she throbbed between her legs, where he ought to be. Her heart pounding in her throat, she grasped his rock hard credentials. He drew in a breath.

"You are a little audacious, are you not?" His words whispered against her skin.

"Am I being too forward?" she said, so nervous that her voice sounded shaky.

"You may be as forward as you please. As you can feel, I am here and ready to serve."

"Should we get this over and done with, quickly?"

"If you want me to please you, we should linger a while over the preliminaries." While he kissed her again, he slipped his hand between her legs.

She whooshed in a breath, desperate to rub herself against him, but he found the tingling place that avoided his touch, but called for gentling all at the same time. Her head thrown back, and breathing through her mouth, she widened her legs, wanting more, wanting less. Then he began sliding himself into her hand. Soon, he would do the same inside her.

She squeezed his velvety steeliness, hoping to guide him into her before she lost her urge, but he didn't take the hint. He continued to tease at her womanly parts until she began seep with moisture. Then he nudged her hand away and found the very most sensitive place between her legs. She bucked every time his fingers passed over, trying to move away. "Let me give you pleasure," he whispered onto her neck.

"Is it pleasure?" She breathed in. "It seems like teasing."

"Only until you reach the peak, but if you don't, that simply means you haven't been taught, or you haven't found out for yourself."

"No one needs to be taught how to make babies. It's

natural." She tensed, trying not to make a sorry spectacle of herself.

"I don't want to make babies, my sweet wife. I want to make love." He rolled her onto her back and separated her legs with his lean hips. "You can stop me any time with a word." He leaned down and kissed her until she responded by hooking her legs across his back. He slid his hands beneath her behind, lifting her higher into him.

"I'm not worrying, Adam," she said, gasping for breath. "So far this is quite interesting, nothing like I imagined. Whatever it is that I am supposed to do ... oh, my lord. That is ..."

He penetrated her, and stilled, with the most enormous cock she could have imagined partway inside her. He breathed softly, while he tickled his lips against hers. Gently, seductively, he eased out and entered again, carefully, until she was certain she couldn't expand any larger. Her breathing turned to gasping, and he stopped again. For no reason she could imagine, she tilted her hips. He let out a sigh of pure pleasure. Why this should be one of the most wonderful moments of her life, she couldn't say. Likely, the wonders of the marriage bed were never properly described in order to discourage females from enjoying themselves without marriage.

Suddenly insecure, she needed him to kiss her again. She sought his lips, and he did so, while he more comfortably entered in and out of her. The rush of sensation caused her to arch against him. When he sped up his movements, she needed to clutch his tight buttocks or be bounced off the bed.

She wanted to laugh or to cry, but instead she sought

and found his mouth again. The intimacy of mouth against wet mouth seemed to fill her needs. Her head arched back and her body tried-tried-tried but couldn't reach the unknown pinnacle she sought. His sweat stuck his body to hers and his heartbeat thudded so strongly that she feared for him. He suddenly clenched the hard muscles of his behind and withdrew from her, and she only minded a little. She had done no more than lie on her back, yet she had loved every minute of the married act. Strangely, she was also exhausted.

She rolled away from him, and the night disappeared as quickly as her virginity had.

The light hadn't yet entered the room when Adam awoke. Soft breezes rustled the leaves outside. From the moment he had opened his eyes, Adam was aware of Cassia in his bed. She breathed regularly, facing toward him, her hand beneath her soft cheek. Last night he hadn't done his lovely virgin bride justice. He should have taken his time, for the moment he had entered her, he had wanted from her exactly the reaction she had given. From there, his eager body had controlled him, with nary a thought of fondling her luscious body until he and she were comfortable enough with each other to laugh and enjoy making love.

Last night was the first time he had made love to a woman rather than joining in erotic pleasuring. He should also pleasure Cassia, and perhaps he should start this morning. Although he didn't doubt that she was entirely virginal, he hadn't noticed any breaking of virginity seals. If he had, she hadn't mentioned any special pain. She seemed to accept the married act as naturally as any woman could. Truth to tell, he had been surprised. Then again, he had surprised himself by getting the whole thing over and done with quickly, as she had suggested.

He glanced at her again in the early morning light. She had worn the same hairstyle to bed as she had worn to her wedding. He had assumed she would brush out her locks or make a sleeping plait. One hairpin had slipped halfway out of the knot at the back of her head. He picked that one off and discovered quite a few more. As he tugged, the weight of her hair unfurled. Fascinated, he watched a pale avalanche slowly tumble down over her face to the pillow. She flicked the curtain of hair from her face. Her eyes slowly opened.

"Good morning, your grace." He stared into her sleepy blue eyes.

"Hmm. Go away."

"Is this how a duchess should greet her duke in the morning?" He sat up, leaning back against the headboard, and crossing his arms over his chest, not sure whether to be annoyed or amused.

"The duchess has never had a husband before, so perhaps she could reconsider. Good morning, duke." She snuggled into her pillow and closed her eyes again.

"Call me Adam." He eyed her. "What should we do today?"

"We should go back to sleep."

"Would I be able to change your mind?"

"No."

He took that as a challenge and slid back down in the

bed. She edged away from him. If his lack of bedroom courtesy last night had decided her she wanted no more of him, he would need to take more time with her this morning. Not being a slick talker like George, he would need to prove he normally left his woman sated. "I have a request."

"Not now, Adam. I want to sleep."

Sighing deeply, he took her into his arms. "And so you shall." He rested her head on his chest, accepting his rejection. When she had slept longer she might be more amenable to making love again.

He had barely closed his eyes when her hand snaked to his hip. Her thumb stroked along the jut of his hipbone. His breath shortened as he tried not to notice that her palm inched toward his groin. His cock rose to attention. He sucked in a breath, his anticipation building. His sweet new bride was no blushing rose. She was determined to do as she chose, when she chose. And with that thought, Cassia closed her hand around his shaft.

He whooshed out a breath. Concentrating on the ceiling, he sweated through her exploration of his length and width. Finally, to encourage her to tighten her hold, he moved his hips. She stared up at him. "Don't you like that?"

"I like that very much, my dear. Let me show you what else I like." Far too urgently, he clasped his hand around hers, tightened her grip and slid it down to his base and back again. He left her to follow his lead, while he tried to think about the pros and cons of the Seditious Meetings Bill currently being discussed in the house of parliament.

Within seconds he had completely lost his concentration. He would finish if he didn't stop her. Breathing hard, he turned into her, and she lost her enthusiastic grip. "Your turn now," he said, his voice unaccountably rough.

He scooped her arm over his shoulder, taking the weight of her breasts into his palms. Careful with the two delicious handfuls, he lowered his head to kiss each pale nipple. Fighting his urgency, he took one lovely bud between his lips while his aching cock pressed against her thigh. Her chest rose and fell with her forced breaths. He pleasured the next nipple while he caressed the first. At last he heard the reaction he had hoped for, murmuring little sounds of pleasure. She grasped the back of his head and wriggled into him.

He nudged her knees apart, his shaft floundered about, hoping for a little guidance from her but she slid her hands down his back, unknowingly stimulating him to bursting point. Rolling on top of her, he rose to his knees. The blankets slipped off and he saw the whole of her upper body. Her nightgown barely covered her soft white shoulders and arms. He grabbed the material and lifted the light linen over her head, breathing hard but somehow managing to control himself.

She had a body as lovely as any he had seen, creamy pale, slim, but curvaceous. "My beautiful Cassia," he said, his voice husky. For she was now his and he would cherish her forever. He tossed her nightgown onto the floor.

Her gaze met his shyly. "My beautiful duke. I do like the way you look without your shirt."

"Then I shall spend the rest of my life without wearing my shirt."

She laughed. "I would be far too distracted if you did, let alone all the other women in London. Best if we keep this between ourselves." Her palm landed on his shaft again. "I mean this, too. If you take another mistress, I shall leave you."

"I will bear that in mind." He dropped over her and kissed her neck, her jaw, her eyes, her forehead, and finally her delicious mouth.

Her hands slid everywhere across his shoulders and back. She drew up her knees either side of his hips. Although he desperately wanted to be inside her, he wanted her to want him there, so he teased her little bud until she thrashed about, hot and wet. Not entering her was torture and a man could only last so long, but he needed control this time. Finally she took his shaft and rubbed him in her wetness. As a blushing bride, she certainly didn't blush. "You are very bold," he said, having to force his voice through his constricted throat.

"Isn't this what you would want?"

"It is exactly what I would want. I'm afraid that I will be spending most of this next week in bed enjoying you."

Her eyes half closed as she arched into him.

Her willingness touched him. A deep emotion swelled inside him, an ache of barely remembered tenderness. He promised himself that he would never hurt her. Although he had to hold back and enter and withdraw a number of times, she finally expanded. Even then he was careful not to overtax her. Any effort on his part, or by his part, would be worthwhile as long as he could keep this woman happy.

In the aftermath, as they lay side by side, sated, he realized he had never had a woman as resilient or as perfect for him. He didn't regret for one minute that his thoughtless words to Lucien had caused the shed door to be locked.

Cassia hadn't expected too much of her wedding night, but Adam's sleepy smile in the morning caused her to stay in bed longer than she normally would, talking about the tasks she expected to do during the day. Being carefully treated to a morning gossip somewhat eased her mind, and dulled the soreness she experienced from the night before.

After he had dressed and left, Cassia rang for Elsie, who had apparently been awaiting a call. She entered the room, creeping about as if she didn't want to awaken a spider, a few of which resided on the windows. Cassia beckoned her into the dressing room. She had already washed in the bathroom and put on fresh underwear, and she wore her dressing robe on top of her chemise. "I plan to wear my pink gown today."

Elsie nodded and looked around for Cassia's stays. Without words, the maid began to dress her.

"Have you always been a kitchen maid?" Cassia asked the girl, who appeared to be about her own age but a head shorter.

Elsie smiled, showing her large square teeth in a surprised smile. She took the pink gown from the rack. "I have been a kitchen maid, but here, I'm an all purpose maid. We all are, ma'am. We've never been put to jobs of our own, not here, not since the duke's parents died. We all help everywhere."

"While I'm here, I will want a ladies' maid. You seem to be quick with the hooks and I'm sure you can pack my gowns away efficiently. Do you think you can dress my hair?"

"I would certainly like to try, ma'am, but the only style I know is the knot." Elsie indicated her own straight dark hair.

"If you work out well, I will have you taught various styles. I can only do the knot too, or a plait. Together we'll work out something. Your job for now is to take care of my clothes and my dressing. I'll keep Flossie in the kitchen. I may have to ask the duke to have more servants sent from the city."

"Thank you, ma'am." Elsie performed a quick curtsey. She began to tidy the slightly disordered room, which might have been reasonably tidy but for the disordered bed. Cassia left the room, determined not to be embarrassed.

Now neatly dressed, Cassia hastened down to the breakfast parlor. Huntsdale would surely want breakfast before he did whatever he planned to do during this stay, and the cook was certainly no cook. She rang the bell and ordered scrambled eggs, bacon, stewed rhubarb, toast, and tea, a wholesome meal but far from splendid. The butler was sent off to find the duke and breakfast began in leisurely fashion. Adam was inclined to be indulgent and pleased with the most everyday things. "I haven't had rhubarb for years," he said, examining his napkin ring, which also appeared to please him.

"We can't have anything but the plainest of menus without a decent cook. Could we have your proper cook sent up, please, Adam?"

"Is my cook not a proper cook?" A crease formed between his eyebrows.

"He is a plain cook. He also is not a Frenchman. As

well, I would like more maids to help in the house. I have taken Elsie as my personal maid."

He creased the expression on his face. "A maid for you. Why did Cedric not think of that? We certainly are a pack of crusty bachelors, not giving a thought to your requirements." His shoulders lifted and a rueful expression crossed his face. "When we get back to town, tell the housekeeper what you need."

"Thank you. I am delighted to be in charge of my life again. One of the benefits of marriage." She smiled into his eyes.

He averted his gaze to his plate. "Have you found any others yet?" he asked in a polite voice.

Her cheeks warmed. "I'm sure I have no need to answer that question."

He raised his head, his mouth widening into a gleaming smile.

She knew exactly why she had been so set against him. He could relax her far too easily. She had never imagined that love might come with marriage but she rather thought she could fall in love with him. Far from being arrogant womanizer, he was a slightly wary, but all too stimulating companion.

But she had never been impressionable and she didn't plan to let down her guard quite yet.

By the end of the next day, Cassia had a complement of servants to run the house efficiently enough for two. The food she had ordered from London had arrived not long after noon with the extra servants, and Adam's town cook had started in the kitchen. Apparently, he could be spared as Jeremy didn't often eat at home. The few open rooms had been fully cleaned and the cobwebs had been removed. Tomorrow the silver would be polished and she would finally have flowers inside the house. The last would be her job, for as yet she hadn't explored the enormous garden.

After another cautious night with her husband, learning more about her body and his, she decided that being married to George would never have suited her. Even now, she didn't like to think of the intimate aspects of marriage with him. If she had ever realized how enjoyable a physical union could be, she would have known that George wasn't for her. Not that he had no joy in him. He simply didn't have the physical appeal for her that Adam had possessed from their initial meeting. Finally she could admit to herself that he had sent her pulses thudding from the first time he had glanced at her. His assessing gaze had connected to her soul.

Had it not been for George telling her Adam had a mistress, she could have been receptive to his courting, instead of instantly defensive. The man was quite perfect, surely, now that he had broken with the other woman who Cassia tried to put out of her mind.

"Your Grace?"

She glanced at the maid, who held her refurbished blue gown for her to step into. "Thank you, Elsie."

"This is such a pretty gown."

"I'm glad you think so. I have been told that blue is not my color, so we altered the binding on the bodice so that the blue doesn't make my complexion too pink."

Elsie's big square teeth showed in a delighted smile. "I do like colors, your grace. I rarely wear them myself because of my grey uniform but some colors seem better on some people than on others."

"One needs the right sort of eye to know that, Elsie, and if you do, you could be the perfect maid for me, a person who doesn't."

After staring at herself in the dressing room mirror, wearing the floral close to her face, she realized that blue was as truly deadly on her as she had imagined. Today she looked light and happy. Because of the floral, her skin glowed. When she had been younger, her mother had loved dressing her in blue to match her eyes, but she doubted her eyes needed to be matched. Everyone didn't have to be pretty, but she looked fresher when her skin tones were not contrasted with blue.

She jammed her shady hat onto a hairdo that would surely collapse before the hour was up, her hair being heavy, unlike most people with her coloring. Elsie had managed a twist that ended with curls on the top of Cassia's head. Never mind. The hat would contain the topple, and she would experiment with another style later. Honeymoons were more than useful to a woman who preferred to be out of society's sight while she changed from a daughter into a wife.

Mrs. Giddings gave her flower shears and a basket. Nearby the house, edged by rolling green lawns, Cassia found the early roses for the vases. The spring growth was beginning, but flowers had not been a priority in this garden. Perhaps the design was better kept big and green with shrubs and trees. She couldn't wait to see Adam's town garden, which he had told her had been started by his mother, who according to his account, had been sweet and delicate. Cassia would never be sweet and delicate. Lemons were neither delicate nor sweet but a person could make lemon cordial with a touch of sugar. If Adam supplied the sugar, Cassia would be sweet. Giving her responsibility was the very way to sweeten her. Without a doubt, she could grow to enjoy her husband very much.

Her basket of flowers swinging, she walked along the slate path back to the house. For a moment, she paused to inspect the view, spotting the Gerard family's gray stone house in the distance. The two properties shared a boundary, visibly divided by a thick growth of trees. A flicker of white caught her gaze. The next movement showed her Adam's broad shoulders. She left her basket and walked toward him. Hunkered on his knees, he didn't notice her coming. She noted a rock that came flying out of the space between a tall oak and a hedge. Then another. He seemed absorbed in his task.

As she stepped close enough for him to hear her voice, she called, "Have I married a laborer?" She glanced at the coat and waistcoat he had left hanging on nearby branch.

He glanced up in her direction, an easy smile crossing his sweaty face. "A mere laborer? I would call myself a builder."

"What are you building?"

He used the sleeve of his shirt to wipe his face. "The stream blocks here in winter when the twigs catch on the rocks. I thought it was time I shifted the rocks so that the water could run easily."

She stared at his arrangement. "Perhaps you should call

yourself a stone mason. That looks very professional." Either side of the curve, he had piled four layers of rocks to contain the steady flow of the stream.

"Look closer," he said, with an assessing glance at her.

She took two steps and he pulled her into his arms. "Never interrupt a stone mason while he is working." His warm breath brushed across her ear. "Or you will have to pay the toll."

She wound her arms around his neck, her heart thudding against his hard chest. Unable to resist, she tangled her fingers in the thick hair at the nape of his head. His eyes turned a smoky blue. His mouth lowered to hers. One soft kiss and he leaned back against his low wall and sat on the top, all very well, but he pulled her with him. Her knees landed either side of him in a very unladylike fashion. "You can't be thinking of doing this here?" She hoped she sounded sensible, because her reaction was anything but. Her heart beat so hard that she could barely breath.

His intense gaze narrowed. He scooped his hands under her skirts, which had settled like a tent around them. "Here, there, and everywhere." His mouth tickled across hers as he undid the flap of his trousers. The very thought of what she was about to do, and where, made Cassia tingle with excitement, which turned into an aching throb when he used his hand to tease between her legs. Within moments she experienced the wetness he had caused last night, lifted slightly, wriggled, and he slowly eased inside her.

Never had she expected marriage to be so wondrous. Even when her hat fell off and her hair covered her back like a curtain, she laughed with enjoyment. Somehow, she had a womanly power over this large and autocratic man. He took far longer this time to reach his stopping point, which was perhaps why she became frantic in her movements, noisy and begging for she didn't know what. When he withdrew, she stayed, her head on his shoulder, aware of the strong rhythm of his heartbeat. He held her, placing a soft kiss on her face. Perhaps she loved him at that moment.

She loved him quite a few more times as the rest of her honeymoon week flew by. Finally, she left for London with him as his new bride. At last, she would be the mistress of her own house.

Before she could receive morning callers, she needed to have the house properly cleaned from top to bottom. She needed to have the rooms aired, the extraneous furniture removed, have the linens inspected, the silver cleaned, and the servants repurposed. Over the next month, many callers would expect cakes and tiny sandwiches from the new bride, and she would be expected to present her own cards to various members of society. She had followed this routine in Surrey and she was now in her element, not the daughter of the house but the lady again. As the wife of a duke she would have many more responsibilities than she had ever had.

No one could have been more pleased than she.

Chapter Ten

In her new townhouse, Huntsdale House, Cassia had an enormous dressing room. She had shelves for her hats, hooks for her coats, a drawer for her gloves, and even a place for her reticules. Her parasols had a place too, but her single one had to survive alone, looking dejected in the tall corner stand. Adam's space wasn't entirely filled either. Many of his shelves held cricket outfits, old hunting jackets or articles that had clearly been folded away many years before. She lifted an increasing pile of discards onto the bed.

"Are you tossing out Adam?" His brother Jeremy stood in the open doorway, his shoulders rested against the side, grinning. "What has he done to deserve this treatment?"

She laughed. Her brother-in-law was a delightful young man who didn't have a serious bone in his entire body. He would make some lady a totally irresponsible husband. "I'm only tossing out the clothes he set aside. I'm sure some needy people will be grateful."

"Oh, you're one of those, are you?"

"One of what?"

"A do-gooder."

"Well, I don't intend to be a do-badder. There are enough of you."

"What have I done that is bad?"

"Nothing, literally."

He stared at her. "Is that the way you try to charm people into liking you?"

"I'm not famous for my charm, as you so rightly point out. I have been here three days and all you have done so far is watch me change everything around, first the servants, then the furniture, and now me getting rid of unwanted goods."

"I fear you might throw me out, too." Jeremy flashed his mischievous smile. "Since I'm useless."

Cassia straightened and placed her fists on her hips. "In that case, perhaps you should make yourself indispensible to me."

"What would you want me to do?" He sounded defensive and folded his arms across his chest.

She liked Jeremy who, at twenty-two years of age, was still a bouncy lad, happy to be friendly with everyone, and without a care in the world. "Dear sweet Jeremy. Would you take this mountain of clothes, along with any you don't currently wear, to the home for the destitute in Whitechapel?"

He heaved a sigh. "Give me an hour and I will. What are you planning for the rest of the day? To re-plant the garden?"

"I haven't decided what to do there, yet. Today, the

Graces are paying me a call. They left a card yesterday. I expect everyone else will do the same next week, which is why I want the house set to order before then."

"At the rate you are going, you will have the house redecorated in another hour. Did I see a new cook in the kitchen?"

"A real French chef. And two more kitchen maids, a parlor maid, a housemaid, and a footman who will start next week. Mr. Rogers will be interviewing another butler today. I think the footmen need someone to keep them better organized."

He looked wary. "What are you planning to do with our old butler?"

"You may not have noticed, but he left two days ago. He decided he would be happier elsewhere."

"Very tactful of him to say so. I doubt that I will miss him. I suspect that many a good bottle of brandy left by the way of his door. I'd best go through my wardrobe as instructed." With an overdone flourish, he turned and made his way back to his rooms on the other side of the landing.

She wondered why he appeared to do nothing all day. Before she had married Adam, she would have presumed the same about him, but he worked very hard keeping his various estates in order. He spent most of the day studying papers on his desk. She had seen him as a wealthy do-nothing, as George had been. However, the week off Adam had taken for his honeymoon had reinvigorated him, or so he said. In her opinion, he didn't need too much more reinvigorating. He managed to keep her occupied in bed night after night. Not that she minded. She wondered how married people managed to fit in their normal daily routines with all the bedroom sports in which they participated.

Once again she thought about Adam's statement before the first time he had bedded her. He'd mentioned she might have discovered something about the married act, or she may have already learned whatever the something might be for herself. If Nora hadn't gone back to Sussex, she could have asked her, though perhaps not, for she was her father's wife. The only person who might tell her whatever she needed to know was Amelia, whom she hoped would continue being her friend.

Cassia didn't normally latch onto someone the way she had to Amelia. The other woman appealed to her, perhaps because of her thoughtfulness or the way she considered before she spoke. Cassia herself tended to be a little tempestuous, and Amelia appeared to be her foil. Others let Cassia have her head, for Cassia had decided opinions on most subjects. Amelia saw the other side that Cassia hadn't considered. She liked that she could possibly learn to be more reasonable with encouragement.

Perhaps Amelia would come to call next week, for as well as personal advice, Cassia needed extra fashionable morning gowns and evening wear. Her few country outfits had been all very well for her brief sojourn in London and her even briefer honeymoon, but were clearly inadequate for a duchess who would be expected to make morning calls as well as attend many evening events. Fortunately, Adam had allotted her an allowance that would cover not only all her expense, but also the sorts of gowns she had only ever envied on others.

After both dressing rooms were put in order, she visited the kitchen where the new cook presided. A real Frenchman with dark hair, a sweaty face, and a loud voice, he already had the two new kitchen maids scuttling around washing plates and stocking the scullery. "You will have small cakes ready for my callers, won't you?" Cassia asked pleasantly, noting that the makings of a midday repast had been set on the central table.

The cook inclined his head. "Already in ze oven, your 'ighness. 'ow many for luncheon? Mr. Jeremy comes and goes. Just you and the master and Mr. Rogers?"

"Prepare for four, as usual."

Cassia backed out, knowing any extra food wouldn't go to waste, now that she had ample servants. When she started, the new housekeeper would see to the menus in future. She hurried through a corridor that needed a coat of fresh paint, to the formal rooms. Adam disliked his workday interrupted but the man needed to be interrupted now and then. After squaring her shoulders, she marched into his study. A few unneeded items, like boxing gloves, rare old bottles of wine, worn cushions, a stack of books, a dried-up inkpot, and a chair with a wobbly leg cluttered the area. She would like the whole room repainted as well, and new curtains at the wide windows, but that may have to wait at least until the end of her first month as the new duchess.

"May I be of some help?" he asked, politely.

The Duke of Huntsdale was not the man who had been with her day and night during her honeymoon. This man was a serious, rather frowning person who had explained to her that his study was sacred. "Indeed you may." She stood in front of his desk, hands clasped in front, like a servant applying for a job. "The Graces will be visiting with their daughters this afternoon. I hope you will join us in the sitting room."

"I don't mean to be impolite, Cassia, but for me this is a normal working day." He rested his pen on his blotter.

"And I would like to show them over the house. Lady Grace says she hadn't seen the rooms since your mother died. She might have a few ideas as to refurbishing."

"Are you asking my permission?"

"Should I be doing so?" She lifted her eyebrows, trying to give him the impression that asking him permission to perform her role was a waste of his time and hers.

"Certainly not. This is your home." He heaved a breath and laid his pen sideways across the papers on his desk, as if preparing for a long and tedious conversation. Meanwhile, he didn't invite her to take a seat.

"I will be showing them an enormous hallway, a gracious drawing room, and a largely unused dining room. I will be showing them inadequate servants' quarters."

"The servants' quarters are more than adequate and not for public viewing." His fingers tapped on his desk.

"It may not have come to your notice, but you have extra maids and you are about to have a new butler who will expect quarters the size of the rooms Mr. Rogers occupies."

His gaze met hers. "I'm hardly about to move Cedric so that I can have a different butler."

"If you move Cedric, you can have a different butler and an almost happy wife."

"Do you dislike Cedric?"

"Of course not. Why can Cedric not have a set of rooms on the second floor? At this time, they are unused."

"Perhaps you could fill them with your new maids." His fingers began tapping again.

"I can find room for them downstairs with the other servants." She left her eyebrows raised, willing him to agree with her.

He leaned back, his face hard. "You will not reorganize my life."

"You reorganized mine." She folded her arms, determined to stand her ground.

His gaze fixed on hers and his expression changed from annoyed to watchful. "Not intentionally."

She crossed her arms. "I was set to marry George and live in Sussex. I am now living in London, far from the only family I have. But you chased me into a feed shed and now I'm married to you. I call that having my life reorganized." She tilted up her chin and set her mouth into a firm line.

For a brief moment, his gaze dropped. Then his shoulders relaxed slightly. "I see." He drew a deep breath and stared at his fingers, which he slowly relaxed. "You want me to shift Cedric."

"I think he will find his private life will be less disrupted if his living quarters are distanced from the servants. He is your assistant and deserves a life of his own. You also have a wife who will be organizing many social activities and needs the extra servants available to help."

"Jeremy and I have never bothered about having social functions in this house."

"I'm sure your mother did."

He kept his focus on her face while he considered, and

then he nodded. "Get the footman to shift Cedric but please let him know what you plan to do, first."

"And you will come out of this room when the Graces arrive?"

Adam sighed. "My idea isn't to live in your pocket, Cassia."

"I have noticed." Cassia gave him an eyelash-batting glance before leaving. But she carefully closed the doors behind her. Now she had her way, she needn't annoy him so often.

Although not immediately, Adam noted that Cedric enjoyed having his own private spot where he could entertain if he pleased. For a single horrifying moment during the conversation with Cassia, he thought she had discovered that being locked in the hayshed had been no accident. His blood had frozen. What had appeared incidental to him *had* changed her life. Fortunately, she knew no such thing.

He didn't obtain any enjoyment from lying to her, but a misunderstanding over which he had no control had happened. The event would be forgotten, and one day he and she would reminisce about that night and laugh.

Being married suited him. Cassia had made a difference to the look of the house. She had opened a few windows, letting in the floral scents of spring. Each room seemed larger and brighter. The servants' quarters had been reconfigured. The new chef had decided to re-train the old cook so that he could find another job rather than stay as an undercook, not that Huntsdale cared either way. However,

Cassia liked him to know her new arrangements, and he ought to listen to her on the odd occasion regarding household matters.

Tonight, a little over three weeks after arriving back in town, she had organized a dinner for the older members of the Gerard family to thank them for their hospitality to her while she had been husband-hunting. The newest footman ushered the guests into the sitting room, and one of Cassia's many arrangements appeared to have escaped his notice. George turned up, clearly invited. Since Jeremy had decided to stay home, George's arrival meant an extra male at the table. Adam raised his eyebrows at his lovely wife, sidling up to her. "The numbers, my dear."

She gave him a wide-eyed smile. "I asked Amelia too," she whispered to him, "but she has a headache and couldn't leave the house."

Adam's face froze. Amelia, at least, understood a reasonable code of behavior. He couldn't have a kept woman at the same table as the leaders of society. Clearly few people knew about her and he would prefer matters to stay that way. Sir Waldo and Lady Gerard had accepted her, but they didn't know what Adam did. Bertie knew, but he wouldn't say a word to his sister Cornelia, and her friend, Essie Deering, the last invited to even up the numbers. Bertie clearly didn't disapprove of that young lady's inclusion. He stared at Miss Deering, so clearly smitten that he made others smile, too.

During the course of the evening, Adam discovered that Cassia meant to have the hall painted in red. George guffawed. "You always said you wouldn't be one to paint the town red and now you plan to do just that."

"Not the whole town, George," she said, patting his hand. "Only the hall. It's huge and can stand the color." She had seated him on her left and they'd been gossiping for some time until George's laugh allowed Adam, at the other end of the table, to overhear part of the conversation.

"This is what comes of not always listening to one's wife," Adam said, disgruntled, turning to Lady Gerard who sat on his right. "You find out you are about to have a red hall."

"Which will look most fashionable, I'm sure. But, Adam, Sir Waldo would be the first to advise a young married man to listen to his wife, wouldn't you, my love?"

"If you don't, more than hallways will be painted red, my lad. Before you can wink, she'll have the whole house rearranged, not that young Cassia hasn't almost done so. I like this dining room. Always did. Your mother used to have some rip-roaring dinners in the old days." Sir Waldo nodded at his wife. "We were lot younger then."

Lady Gerard leaned forward to smile at Cassia at the other end of the table. "It's so sweet of you to have us as your first dinner guests, Cassia."

"You are my experiment with the new chef. Someone had to be sacrificed." Cassia's grin was not only mischievous, but also charming. Adam couldn't have been more proud of his young wife, or any more ridiculously besotted. New toys were invariably more entertaining than the old.

When Cassia's maid, Elsie, came to help undress her later in the night, he dismissed her. "We won't need you to undress the duchess while I am at home," he told the woman. She blushed hotly and backed out.

"That was rather high-handed of you," Cassia said as

she tried to unfasten her pearl necklace. "I prefer to deal with my maid myself."

"Husbands have certain rights. I take the undressing of my wife seriously." He frowned but fortunately she wore a slightly amused expression. Somewhat relieved, because had no intention of being a tyrant, he strode into his own dressing room and returned with the velvet box he had wanted to give her since before his wedding. The time had never been right to present her with the family jewels. A gift from him was a different matter from officially recognizing her as his duchess and rather more significant. She would then be completely his. He stood in front of her with the velvet box in his hands. "I was going to give this to you before dinner but I didn't think you would want to wear it with that gown."

"Why wouldn't I?"

"It's rather showy and your gown doesn't want something showy with all those white roses around the neckline. Your pearls look better."

"Perhaps I need not employ Amelia if you know so well what goes with what." She grinned mischievously. "Let me see what you have there."

He opened the case that held his mother's diamond set, watching her expression while she took her time staring at finest stones money could buy.

She inhaled deeply. "My goodness. I don't know where I would wear that, but certainly not for a friendly dinner."

"We'll find numerous occasions during which you will be able to wear this and the rest of the set in the tray beneath." He waiting, hoping she liked diamonds.

"They're lovely, Adam." She edged aside the box so that

she could throw her arms around his neck and lift her lovely face. "Thank you."

He held her with one arm, and with the other he shut the box and tossed the set onto the bed.

That night, he slowly undressed her, garment by garment, enjoying every button, every hook, every lace. When the carpet lay littered with a jumble of his and her clothes, he participated in a night of lovemaking he would never forget.

And she hadn't even glanced more than once at the diamonds.

Two days later, with the public rooms in Huntley House mainly set in order, Cassia paid a call on Amelia, who looked very beautiful standing in the doorway of her small house with a surprised smile on her face.

"I've missed you, Amelia." Cassia leaned forward to place a kiss on her friend's cheek. "I thought you would come to call on me, but since you didn't ..."

Amelia took a deep breath. "I'm a working woman, Cassia." She took both Cassia's hands in hers. "I don't pay morning calls on duchesses unless I am asked in a professional capacity."

"I certainly want to employ you, but I don't quite know how to separate your working life from your private life. Professionally, Adam wants me to have many more evening gowns. I'm not to spare any expense, which means I can pay for speedy deliveries. You are my best, in fact, only adviser, though Adam tries to hint which gowns of mine he doesn't like. And he is not too subtle, either." She laughed.

"Come inside." Amelia led her into her tiny sitting room. "If I am speaking to you as a friend, Cassia, I can tell you that you don't need me professionally. You only need to see Mrs. Gordon. She knows whom you married, and the size of the pockets she will try to empty. She will show you her book in which she has pictures of the latest Paris fashions. She can make any of them for you as speedily as you like, knowing you can now afford her to employ extra seamstresses." She swept her arm across the room, indicating Cassia could sit wherever she wished.

Cassia perched on the front of an armless chair. "That's where I fall down. I don't know what suits me."

"She would be happy to hold colors under your chin and let you see what is best for you and she will also give you her opinion." Amelia sat opposite her in the matching chair and folded her hands neatly in her lap. "That's how she makes her living."

Cassia stared at her feet. She couldn't help but note that Amelia was trying her level best to be rid of her. "This is why I also need you as a friend. I trust you. You know I do."

"You have as little reason to trust me as you do to want me as your friend."

"I'm very opinionated, Amelia. I never imagine I need a reason to trust someone and choose her as a friend. I think my instinct serves me very well. I liked you from the start and you have never let me down."

"But you know nothing about me." Amelia's expression flattened.

"How much do you know about me?"

"I know you are honest and forthright. I know you are kind."

"I know all that about you, too. I want those traits in my friends. When they have those traits, I trust them."

Amelia dragged in and let out a long breath. "Oh, Cassia. How can I resist accepting your friendship when you bolster me with such supportive words? There's no denying that I would love to go with you to Mrs. Gordon's and help you choose your gowns."

Cassia's heart lightened. "And the best part is that Adam gave me my own brougham. I can use it any time. It's one of the Huntsdale carriages, in the Huntsdale colors, just like the one you had. The driver wears a similar uniform, but I expect most do."

Amelia blinked. "As long as they look clean and neat, I don't particularly notice the uniforms of drivers."

"So, now I can share mine with you as you shared yours with me. Without thinking."

"It was simple enough." Amelia's cheeks turned pink. "I didn't have to pay for either the brougham or the driver."

"It was no less generous for that. Anyhow, I'm not planning on shopping today. I simply wanted to see you, because you are my friend."

"And because you are mine." Amelia's eyes glossed slightly.

"Amelia, please, come to call on me. I would love to show you my new home and share my ideas for changes with you. It's no use talking to Adam about household matters, because he assumes I know everything there is to know about households. It's a great responsibility, being a duke's wife, a far greater responsibility than it was being my father's daughter. If I wasn't right, or I didn't know how to manage certain tasks, my father would take over."

"I see your husband as being a managing sort of man. I'm surprised he doesn't want to take over too."

"I think I'm his new toy. He doesn't want to break me." Cassia smiled.

"He sees you as a toy?"

"Hmm. You know he had a mistress, don't you?"

Amelia's back stiffened and her cheeks turned pink. "I'm not a member of society. I don't know who has a mistress or who does not."

Cassia hoped she hadn't embarrassed the other woman. "I believe it's not so rare, but he has me now, and, hmm."

"Is her existence worrying you?" Amelia asked in a strained voice.

Cassia sighed. "He is ... hmm."

"Demanding?"

"Not at all. I can't quite catch up to him. He knows more than I do about ... *that.*"

"*That*?" Amelia's widened and her mouth took on a tiny curve. "I should think he would."

"You were married, and I need to ask someone who has been married about the married act." Cassia caught and held Amelia's gaze. "He is rather ardent."

"You could try telling him *no* and see if he takes notice of you."

"He does when I tell him *no*, or would if I did tell him *no*. I'm too busy saying *yes, yes, yes*. I'm not at all a delicate bride. I enjoy being bedded."

Amelia's smile reached her eyes and she made a sound like giggle. "I'm so glad for you. What did you want to ask?"

"I think I'm not matching up to his mistress. He makes love to me until he reaches his peak but I don't seem to reach mine. If that is the lot of a woman, I will have to bear it, but he said something, I can't remember his exact words, but somehow I'm supposed to end like him, but I don't." Cassia put her hands to her cheeks to try to cool her embarrassment.

Amelia dropped her focus on Cassia's face. "I didn't either in the beginning of my marriage, until suddenly I did."

"For no reason?"

Amelia raised her gaze. "My husband and I were not experienced. In the beginning, neither of us knew any more than you do. But I always had a feeling, like you, that there should be more. It is not connected to ... oh, dear. I have never discussed this before." She planted a palm on each of her cheeks as if to blot up the heat. "It's a matter of your pleasure spot," she said in a low voice. "When it is stimulated, you find pleasure."

"He does that, but still I don't."

"Be patient, Cassia. If he is an experienced lover, he will want your satisfaction too. It will happen, I promise you."

"I hope I didn't embarrass you by asking." Cassia could hardly believe she had asked, but now the words had been spoken, she realized that sharing an intimate detail of her life was completely new to her. Somehow, Amelia's frank answer brought them even closer together.

"You did a little, but the least women can do for each other is share our knowledge. We shouldn't all have to reinvent the wheel."

"I wonder if my mother would have discussed this with

me if she hadn't died so young." Cassia leaned back in the chair, wondering.

"I don't think mothers discuss this, no. I think it is a discussion for friends."

"And we are friends, aren't we?"

Amelia nodded. "We are. Let's plan our shopping day."

"Is tomorrow too soon?"

Amelia smiled. "Do you have an allowance or does the duke pay your bills?"

"I have a very generous allowance. But although I like having a rich husband, I am not in the habit of wasting money, and I doubt that it will become a habit. I keep thinking of economies when I don't need to think of economies. I know we should employ as much staff as we need to run the house, but I don't see the point of buying any more household goods when Adam already so many. And the wedding presents are still rolling in. I wonder how long I need to keep the extra china before I find more suitable housing for it?"

"Perhaps you should keep the extras for your children."

"I wouldn't want to do that when people need my surpluses right now. Jeremy thinks I am a do-gooder, but I don't like to see people in need when I never have been."

"You're not a do-gooder. You're a re-houser." Amelia's eyes twinkled. "I don't think you should give away wedding presents, Cassia. Or at least not for the first year."

"See? These are the things I don't know and the reason why I need a friend. I'll call for you tomorrow at ten." Cassia stood, and she left after kissing her friend on the cheek.

She disliked keeping her driver waiting for her, or not so

much the driver, who at least had shade, as the poor horses, which had to idle in the weather, flicking blown leaves off their irritable ears.

Her driver, Max, drove her back to the same house at ten the next day. Amelia was waiting, dressed beautifully in a dark blue pelisse that dramatized her huge brown eyes. She wore a delicious matching hat on her fashionably styled hair. The color showed off her hair as the most sophisticated auburn one could imagine.

Elsie had done her best with Cassia's hair, but the weight made forming curls difficult. Again she wore a plaited knot. She also wore a sweet little carnelian necklace that she had inherited from her mother.

"That carnelian is lovely with your pretty amber pelisse, Cassia," Amelia said as she settled in the carriage. "Don't tell me you don't understand colors because you do."

"I understand colors except in relation to me. Elsie, my maid, chose the necklace. Last night, Adam presented me with all the jewelry his mother owned. She was very grand. I won't find the time to wear half of them."

"I think he is very much in love with you, Cassia."

"Do you?" Strangely, Cassia hadn't considered this. She frowned. "He has never said so but I think we have a very companionable marriage. He leaves me to do as I wish, which I think my father found to be a good idea, too. Except for Adam's awkward idea of chasing me into the feed barn before we were married, he hasn't put a foot wrong." Since Amelia knew nothing about the feed barn incident, Cassia's cheeks heated a little. "I trust him. If it weren't for the fact that he had a mistress, I would think he was rather perfect."

"Men will be men." Amelia clasped her hands and stared at her fingers.

The carriage clipped past Green Park. Cassia wondered if she should explain about her forced marriage but decided to leave matters where they stood, with Amelia assuming the marriage had been one of mutual convenience. "I doubt my father had a mistress and he was alone for many years before Nora came along." She stopped and considered her words, knowing Amelia was in almost the same position as Nora before marriage. "And it was fortunate he did because she was a struggling widow with two young sons. My father didn't take advantage of her. He married her."

"Some men do the right thing instantly. Others are not so clear headed. A widow's lot is not easy, to which I can attest."

"That's the bad part, Adam taking advantage of the woman's lack of protection." Cassia glanced at the passing scenery, the tree lined streets, the gleaming horses, and the polished brass fittings on the carriages. The sky gleamed a dusky blue and wispy clouds streaked the sky.

"He gave her his protection," Amelia answered in a low voice. "Not many women have young, rich, and handsome lovers. I would say that they must have been fond of each other. A man as well endowed as he, could take his pick of women."

Cassia closed her eyes, momentarily, knowing she had trapped Adam by her foolish decision to go outside when she should have remained with the others inside. "In that case, I was doubly lucky, wasn't I?" Her eyes prickled, but she swallowed any idea of self-pity. Adam had been truly noble to have asked for her hand in marriage when he and she both knew he could take his pick of the younger debutants. He didn't deserve a wife like her who was turning his life upside down to please her own notions of how a ducal residence should be run.

"I think he enjoys a challenge and you challenge him. He's had to work at gaining your attention. I see him as a man who needs an equal partner. The responsibilities of being too rich are great. He needs a woman by his side who can shoulder some of those responsibilities. From the tales you have told me, you are used to running a large household of servants."

"You think he needs a managing sort of woman?" Cassia lifted her eyebrows. "If so, then I was fortunate. I like to organize more than households. I also like to poke my nose into stables to make sure they run efficiently, and I am a martinet in the garden."

Amelia laughed. "I doubt any of that would put him off, Cassia."

Cassia nodded as if she believed Amelia. Adam was occasionally grumpy when she wanted to speak to him about some matter or other. He seemed to think he shouldn't be bothered and, frankly, she only bothered him because she thought most of the decisions she took as hers were his. Her father had told her so whenever she tried to interfere in anything but the running of the kitchen and the design of the garden. He often gave the gardeners orders that conflicted with hers.

The carriage continued into bustling Oxford Street and pulled up in front of the dressmaker's premises. "Let's hope we can get these gowns ordered and out of the way in an hour. I want to look at hats, too." Without waiting for the aid of the driver, Cassia stepped onto the footpath. The morning sun glinted on the glass windows. She held out her hand for Amelia, who followed.

Mrs. Gordon opened the door for her two customers, smiling from ear to ear. "Just the customer I wish to see, Duchess. I have a delivery of a dark green silk that I put aside for you."

Chapter Eleven

Adam arrived home, surprised yet again by the red hall, which even he had to admit looked striking with the black and white marble tiling on the floor. Today, an enormous arrangement of white flowers had been placed on the elegant hall table. The fire-red warmed the area, while outside the weather had moved into a cycle of rainy nights and dry days. If this spring was as wet as the last, his wheat crops would suffer, and he would need to reconsider whether to plant more grain or to expand his stock instead.

Cassia arrived in a hallway from the back of the house, pulling off a pair of dirt-stained leather gloves. "You've been working in the garden," he said, stating the obvious, because she also wore a dirt-stained apron over a dark woolen gown.

"I've been planting cuttings in the flower beds. If we keep the hedges clipped during spring, we will end up with formal walkways. I do like the huge shady tree in the centre. It is a good place to hang lanterns at night. I plan to invite family or friends, or both, to celebrate the season with us. I want the garden to look as pretty as possible by then."

The fact that at her young age, she honestly liked organizing social events amazed him. His mother had complained mightily when she needed to accommodate his father's cronies. Being so attracted to the right woman seemed almost too good to be true for, other than the odd flirtation before Mellie, Adam never really noticed another woman.

He encircled his perfect choice with one arm and kissed her on the mouth. She let her hand linger on his shoulder while he tried not to appear besotted.

If anyone had asked him why he doted on her, he couldn't have managed a coherent answer. Although his thoughts centered on her willowy curves and the fragrance of her skin, he never failed to be attracted to her utter lack of vanity. She poked at that incredible hair of hers without particularly worrying about disturbing the style. She treated the servants with a mixture of respect and authority. Without a touch of shyness about her, or restraint, her kindness showed in her every expression. "In this weather, a small but rowdy dinner with my friends would suit me perfectly."

"The problem is that your rowdy friends are single. This means I either have to be the only woman present or need to invite young ladies to even up the numbers. Then, young ladies need chaperones."

"True enough." He smiled. "You possibly wouldn't want ladies of the night to replace your young lady friends."

"That could be interesting." She gave him a mischievous glance. "Though, I imagine I would then be considered unsuitable as a chaperone myself. I have been thinking about hosting a supper dance. The older people might be amused with card games while the younger people flirt on the dance floor."

"Cedric can organize that for you. No need to trouble your head."

"I would like someone else to do the decorating but organizing is one of my skills. I enjoy putting people together and I love pondering over menus. You have married a frivolous woman, Adam."

He smiled as if he believed her, but a woman with less frivolity about her could not be found. She was the most responsible young lady of his acquaintance. "Hire whomever you wish."

The knocker sounded outside. The footman took his stately time to open the carved wooden door, clearly knowing that most of Adam's friends would stroll inside if left waiting on the doorstep for any length of time. Lucien stepped over the threshold, nodded at the man, and stared accusingly at Adam. "Cards?" He pushed his hands into his pockets and leaned back on his heels, his eyebrows raised in question.

"Cards?"

"Jeremy didn't know your plans for tonight. I said I would find out. Have you forgotten or don't you plan to keep up with your friends now you are a married man?"

Adam blinked. "I had forgotten. Give me a moment to change and I'll be with you." He glanced at Cassia and raced up the stairs, knowing his valet was awaiting him to change for dinner.

Although his normal duties didn't allow him to play

cards every night as some of his friends did, he had visited Whites' once a week for years with his cronies. The only time he had not was during the past month of his honeymoon. In almost no time, he wore an evening jacket, a fresh shirt and cravat. His hat and gloves handed to him, he joined Lucien, who sat with Cassia in the sitting room downstairs. "You don't mind, do you?" he asked her when he saw the blank expression on her face.

"Of course not. I have many tasks to occupy me. When do you think you will be back?"

"No later than midnight."

She nodded and he smiled with relief, hoping Lucien didn't see him as a henpecked husband asking his wife's permission to leave.

Although the meal was ordinary and the card games bored him, being with his peers stimulated him. Apparently, after the foul weather of the past two years, a mild spring season was forecast. He would be pleased not to have his fields destroyed by the frosts again this year. At times, he wondered why he kept trying to hold to his father's plans. If it hadn't been for Cedric Rogers, who had been his father's right hand man, Huntsdale would have thrown in the towel before he turned twenty-two. Only the other man's experience kept Huntsdale on track, his major advice being to keep his textile factory if he wanted a steady income steady when his crops failed.

"I don't know what my father would have done without our sheep this year," George told him during the convivial meal. The usual group sat at the table, including Lucien, Bertie, and Jeremy. "Our silver mines have almost petered out. Fortunately, the copper is carrying us. But when that finishes, we'll have to rely solely on grain. You didn't think I knew that, did you? Well, working for my father has taught me a great deal." He leaned back in his chair, his thumbs hooked into his waistcoat pockets, his expression satisfied. Every day he looked more like his father, a distinguished gentleman with fine skin and graying fair hair.

"I wish I had worked for my father. I had to learn on the job." Adam placed his dinner napkin on the table. "He wanted me to have my years at Oxford more than he wanted me to learn on the job. Perhaps his idea was sound. Having an education helps with my business dealings."

George grinned. "I could have done with one to help me to negotiate with my father. That's why I had to run home before you were married—to negotiate. It seems a housemaid got herself with child."

Jeremy emptied the last of the bottle of Burgundy into his glass. "Women don't usually get themselves with child, George. They seem to need help, or so I have been told by those who don't want my help."

George offered Jeremy a long-suffering glance. "The lad was born with blond hair." He shrugged. "I'm the only man with light hair that Mildred associated with, or so she said. I didn't doubt her." His mouth twisted wryly. "My father was beside himself. He rang a peal over my head, but what else is a fellow to do when he is stuck in the country for weeks on end?"

Adam emptied his glass, ready to begin a convivial game of cards. "Presumably, this is why you have been banished to the city."

George turned to him. "I'm expected to prove I can be

trusted with a little responsibility. I have been told I will support Mildred and the boy on my allowance which will be increased on the same scale as my input." He lifted his shoulders.

Although Adam experienced a certain amount of sympathy, for fathering an illegitimate child was certainly not unknown, George crying poor irritated him. The man had only just begun to apply himself to a task where he need not bend his back, whereas most of the workforce in the country was employed in manual labor. Primary production on farms and pastures kept people eating, and that was one of life's realities. George had only just begun to work and he had a lot to learn, as Adam had after his father died.

His father's and now his factory contributed to employment, not on the same scale as his tenancies but had increased year by year. Rising to his feet, he reached over and clapped George on the shoulder. "A son. Congratulations are in order. I assume you don't intend to marry the mother."

"Not on your life. M'father wouldn't let me even if I did wish to do so. He always thought I would marry Cassia. Now he is against anyone else I may have in mind, not that I do. Have anyone in mind, I mean." His gaze faltered.

Adam nodded. He suspected this. A man who had known Cassia all his life would have elevated opinions of women. No one else would ever be good enough.

Left to her own devices for the first time since her marriage, Cassia sprang into action. During the daylight, she had plenty to occupy her time, what with consulting with the housekeeper on the shifting of furniture from one room to another, trying to work out what looked better where, or what might be charitably disposed of. A few of the old rugs needed replacing, the curtains needed repairs, and the linen closet was a disgrace. At nighttimes, she normally sat and sewed while Adam read one thing or another, mainly pertaining to his holdings. They kept each other company in companionable silence. Tonight, naturally, a meal had been prepared for him. No meal should ever go to waste, nor should her time.

She missed long chats with other women, or working with other women, which she had been wont to do her whole life, either sewing for charities or preserving large batches of food for storage. With so many servants in the house she no longer did the latter. Her charity sewing had become singular. She wondered if city people had the same habits. So far, all she had noted about London women was their constant search for entertainment. In her view, entertainment could also come while sewing and nattering. A good gossip never hurt anyone.

She turned to the footman. "I want a carriage at the front door as soon as possible, please. I will write a note for the driver to deliver."

He nodded and she left for the morning room, which served her as an all-purpose room these days. She read there, she sewed there, and she ate her midday meals on the small round table near the outside door. By the window she had slotted Adam's mother's writing bureau, a delicate mahogany with a piecrust shelf and two long drawers. She dashed off a quick note to Amelia and presented the envelope to the footman.

Within half an hour, Amelia arrived in the carriage, on her face an expression of doubt. Cassia hugged her. "Two women about to have a night without men. What mischief should we get up to?"

"Something incredibly naughty like redesigning a few hats?"

"First, dinner. Adam left at the turn of a heel and I already had a nice meal organized. Jeremy is out, too. I didn't want to eat alone. I'm so glad you could come."

Amelia removed her gloves and sat on the couch beside Cassia. "I eat alone most nights. It was such a pleasant surprise to receive your note."

Cassia rang her hand bell. The meal arrived and was served on her small table. The setting was perfect for two women who simply wanted to gossip. During the meal, they covered garden design, the new gowns that the Gerard girls had worn to the most recent ball, speculation about Essie and Bertie, the likelihood of Jeremy settling down, nil, and George's new role as the manager of his father's shipping company. Cassia laughed. "It's nice to have him living in the city but rather disappointing that he took my marriage to Adam so casually. The least he could have done was look disappointed."

Amelia's forehead creased. "But you weren't in love with him, were you?"

"Never. I thought we might be comfortable together, but now I'm married to Adam, I realize that a marriage to

George wouldn't have suited me one bit, because of the hmm."

"Hmm?"

"Various marital intimacies." Cassia pretended to concentrate on the monogram on the table napkins, a large H entwined with vine leaves.

Amelia placed her knife and fork together, having finished her plate of fricasseed rabbit. "You and George weren't meant to be, which is quite perfect when you are happy with the duke."

Cassia nodded. "Can you imagine marrying again?"

"Sadly, no."

"You must have loved Mr. Gates very much."

Amelia drew a deep breath. "I did, but he died more than three years ago. Aside from that, I find the most unsuitable men to love." She gave a tiny lift of her shoulders.

"Do you find these men very often?"

Amelia smiled. "Rarely. Only the one who is not in a position where he would find marriage to me possible."

"Is there a way to make his position possible?"

Amelia shook her head. Since she had not offered an explanation, Cassia couldn't insist on knowing where the problem lay. Had the man needed a better job or more money, neither would have been insurmountable. Perhaps he had dying parents he needed to care for? Though, surely having a wife would help him in that situation. Any number of reasons could account for not being able to marry a jewel like Amelia. In time, Cassia would discover the problem and do her best not to meddle.

"Well, while I have you to myself, I will ask yet again for

your aid. I'm hoping to hold a supper dance here in few weeks time. You have such wonderful taste that I would be most appreciative if I could hire you to decorate the hall and the ballroom for me. And of course, the tables will have to look quite marvelous for supper. I will be on show as the duke's new wife, and I don't want to let him down."

Amelia drew a long breath. "I would very much enjoy that job."

"Wonderful. Now that's settled, I have a personal favor to ask as well."

"Now that you have buttered me up first." Amelia made a mock-prissy mouth.

"I hoped you would not notice. It occurred to me that now I am married, I make a suitable chaperone for young unmarried ladies. If you could also aid me as a chaperone at the supper dance, I could have your company and find so much more enjoyment in the whole affair."

"Oh, Cassia." Amelia stared at her, blinking with thought. "It is quite some time since I was invited as a guest to a formal affair. People may be shocked to see me when they know I am a working woman."

"People will be overjoyed, if you want my opinion. You dress so tastefully and you will give the ladies a chance to see how smart they could look if they had as much style as you. And you may meet another who could give you reason to say 'phhft' to your beau who can't marry you."

Amelia put her table napkin on the table. "Yes. Yes. This may be a terrible mistake I am making but I would love to help you and also attend your function."

Cassia smiled and rang for the maid to take the plates. "And, of course, that is not all. I know I will meet many other ladies now I am married, but at this stage I only know the adorable Gerards and a few of their immediate friends. I have been accustomed to sitting and sewing babies' clothes to donate to the poor. I know I can take them to the London Hospital but I would like to join a group of ladies who do the same thing. Do you know of one?"

"I'm afraid not, Cassia. I have never done anything charitable myself and I expect I should."

"Good. We shall be the start, then."

"I could tell the other ladies for whom I work about your new sewing group."

"I think we should quaff a glass of sherry to celebrate this momentous day, don't you?" The maid entered the room to take the dishes, and she glanced at Cassia. "Yes, Dora. We will have glasses and a bottle of sherry when you have done that."

"Yes, Your Grace." The maid left with a smile and the plate.

The sherry gave both ladies flushed cheeks and the propensity to giggle. Cassia spent one of the nicest nights since her marriage gossiping about nothing and laughing. She suspected, judging by her father's card evenings, that Adam was doing something similar, with a trifle more alcohol than she and Amelia needed. She went up to bed after Amelia had left in the carriage and slept until Adam arrived home, smelling of cigars and brandy.

He seemed as interested in his marital rights as he always was, but a man couldn't leave his wife at the drop of a hat whenever he pleased. His wife could certainly let him know this. Unfortunately, she couldn't also deprive herself. She discovered that when he needed to try harder to please her that he could be marvelously inventive. That night she experienced her first gloriously unexpected womanly explosion. She almost fainted with the pleasure. "Oh dear," she said languidly as she snuggled into his chest in the aftermath. "Now I shall have to forgive you for leaving me."

He said nothing. The insensitive brute fell asleep. At least he held her in his arms.

Cassia made her list of guests, and her footman delivered the invitations. She had her answer within days, with not a single refusal. "Eighty people, Adam. I hope that is enough for a supper dance." She moved a red velvet cushion behind her back, making herself comfortable on the armless lady's chair, before picking up her embroidery.

Adam nodded. He sat at the end of the settee, his papers in his lap, and his gaze racing over his page. She doubted he was listening. The man worked far too hard. He rarely took time for himself. Her job as his wife was to make sure he did, which was why she was prepared to organize as many social events as she could manage.

"I also invited two donkeys," she added in a companionable voice. "I asked the kitchen cat but unfortunately all she did was turn her back and walk away. I assume she would rather have had a dish of milk. Would you assume that?"

He nodded again, forcing his neglected wife to put her sewing aside, stand, and walk over to him. She carefully removed the pages from his knee, replacing them with herself. "Do you want to know about my arrangements for the supper dance?" She straightened his cravat.

For a moment he looked blank. Then his eyes glossed with the expression she know to be desire. "Only if you want me to know. I'm sure you don't need my input."

"I think we know each other well enough now to have a relationship outside the bedroom."

"But my dear, I cannot strip you naked in the drawing room. Jeremy may arrive home at any time and he will be thunderstruck."

"That's what I mean. You think a relationship consists of being naked together?"

"Only the best relationships."

"You are incorrigible." Although she kept her tone even, she meant her words. The man only took her seriously in the bedroom. Other than that, he appeared to think her life was filled with morning calls and visits to the dressmaker. "What are you reading that is so interesting you need to neglect your wife?"

"Feasibility studies for planting out acres of cherry trees."

"Don't you have enough to do without that?"

"Possibly, but cherry growing is profitable. I wondered how it would be if we concentrated less on the common apple and more on employing workers."

"I should have hoped that when your new wife is sitting on your knee, you would have thoughts other than more money-making ventures."

"And yet, when I had other thoughts, you brought me up short."

"There is no accounting for wives, is there?" She knew

she was being capricious. Moodiness had never been part of her life but when he took no interest in the most important function she had ever planned in her life, she saw herself as superfluous to him. He wanted her to enjoy her life but the sharing of the enjoyment didn't seem to be on his agenda. Farming matters occupied him day and night. "Am I spending too much money?" Staring deep into his eyes, she found those tiny flecks of gold highlights in the cornflower blue.

"I doubt it."

"Do you check?"

"Cedric takes care of expenses. If we had a problem he would let me know."

Now might be the time to tell him that Amelia was helping her. She had put off the subject because he never seemed overly enthusiastic about her friend and she didn't want to see his strange expression whenever she mentioned Amelia's name. Why she wanted him to approve of the woman, she couldn't say. She didn't disapprove of any of his friends, for she liked them all. His gentlemen friends were a tight-knit group, having been brought up together and attending the same schools. Aside from his lighthearted, brother Jeremy, his friend Bertie Gerard was considerate. Lucien was a little more devious than the others, though he had a thoughtful streak. George, of course, was her friend, not to be criticized in any way.

"We haven't had a single refusal. I'm hoping that's not because people want to see if you have married a woman who is good enough for you."

"I never planned to marry a good woman, but I couldn't help myself."

She blinked. She knew that after their night together in the hayshed, he had been forced to propose, but she also knew that he was attracted to her before that, or why else would have been so keen to kiss her whenever he managed to find her alone? Why else would he have so persistently accosted her? "Nevertheless, our marriage has worked out quite well, don't you think?" Her cheeks warmed. She was practically asking for a compliment, which said little for her confidence.

"I'm quite addicted to you, my Cassia. Except when you disturb my papers."

"So, you don't want to know about the arrangements for the supper dance?"

His forehead creased. "Do you need my help?"

"Of course not."

"Then I don't need to know anything."

"Do you assume I am organizing the whole thing myself?"

"Yes. Are you not?"

"Amelia is helping me."

His breathing appeared to still and his expression tightened. "That's very good of her," he said in a voice that sounded forced.

"Why don't you like her?" She dropped her fingers from his collar and squared her shoulders.

"I don't have any feelings for her. I simply think she is not a suitable companion for you."

"Am I allowed to find fault with your friends?" Rising to her feet, she stared down at him.

He held her gaze. "Which of my friends has displeased you?"

"So far, none."

He reached for his papers and put them on his knee again. "If any do, please let me know."

"And what will you do?"

"That depends on why you are displeased with them."

"In other words, you won't do a thing. Well, I want Amelia for my friend, and I expect you to treat her with the same courtesy as you treat your own friends." She folded her arms.

He lifted his eyebrows and gave a curt nod. "I understand. You will forgive me if I don't feel the need to greet her with a kiss?"

Her cheeks froze. "You may kiss whomever you wish to kiss." Her chin high, she strode to the French doors and stared out at the garden. Dusk covered the greenery with a haze of grey. Tomorrow, torches would light the garden for her guests who would be sure to wander outside, if only to see the changes she had made.

"Thank you," he said in a deep growly voice.

She turned to discover that he was again concentrating on the papers on his lap. Apparently, out of bed, she couldn't hold his attention for more than three seconds. She drew a few deep breaths and took her temper back under control. No woman could quarrel with a man who took more interest in fruit growing than in his wife's friends. Nevertheless, she had no inclination that night to sleep in his arms.

The next day, she wondered why she had wanted him to like her friend. After all, the two rarely needed to meet. When Amelia arrived the next morning to begin decorating the ballroom, Cassia took her hands, and leaned forward to kiss Amelia's cheek.

"Oh." Amelia looked surprised but pleased. "Let's hope my arranging will live up to your hopes."

"I have full confidence in you. You will do a wonderful job." Cassia latched onto her friend's arm to walk her toward the drawing room.

Amelia balked. She faced Cassia, her eyes unblinking. "I have done this job previously. Before I decided I would be able to earn an income on my own, I worked as a housekeeper." She stood, her chin up, her expression half defiant, half apologetic.

Cassia took her hands. "I think no less of you, Amelia, if you are imagining you have shocked me. A widow without an income has a hard time supporting herself. If you have a skill you should use it. I'm glad your other skill gave us a chance to meet. Come, let's plan, and then I'll call for the footmen to do as you say."

Chapter Twelve

Adam's guests had arrived in a never-ending stream, and pouring through the entrance hall of his townhouse, enthusiastically gossiping as they filled the ballroom. A hundred people, his wife had said, but they all appeared to arrive at the same moment, exclaiming over the new color of the walls, before congratulating him on his marriage. His fingers had been wrung by proponents of the art, squeezed dry, and dropped. Now, given a moment of relief, he flexed his right hand behind his back.

At least forty times he was told how pleased his guests were to see Huntsdale House opened up again. Since the death of his parents, no one other than his old friends had been through this newly refurbished hall. With the doors of the ballroom opened out into the reception area, the slow wail of a violin being tuned warned that soon the musicians would be drowning out the conversations.

Somehow, Cassia already had everyone lined up for a

country-dance. He wished he had listened to her, for he had no idea of the order of the night, if she had an order, which he suspected was far more than likely. His wife was a very organized woman. Those who didn't plan on dancing this set moved to the sides of the room to gossip. Seeing the hall full and the lingerers surging forward, he remembered seeing the ballroom holding a far larger crowd. Cassia had been wise to limit her guest list for her first function.

He noted Amelia speaking to Lady Gerard and wished he could be more welcoming to the beautiful widow, but keeping a polite smile on his face when he spoke to her was as much as he could manage. She shouldn't be here, and if his wife knew who she was, likely she wouldn't be. But his willful Cassia was determined to hold to her own opinions. He had tried to warn her off the woman more than once, and failed. He could only hope reality would treat her kindly.

Before he could be roped into dancing with one of her young guests, he escaped into the dining room, which Cassia had designated the supper room. The doors had been set back into the walls and the cold dishes had already been set out. A footman stood ready to take empty plates back to the kitchens. Already a few of his bachelor friends had lined up.

"If you eat this food you are expected to dance with the young hopefuls," he said in a mock stern voice to Rodney Toddington, a tall young aristocrat with dark curly hair and a shy manner.

"It would be my pleasure, d-duke." Rodney offered a smile full of charm. "I only need to eat so that I can keep up my energy for d-dancing."

"Mmmff," Lucien said, his mouth stuffed full. He swallowed. "None of us minds having our arms full of women. So few old biddies and so many young beauties here tonight. How fortunate we got you married off first to a woman who enjoys the social whirl."

"You had a hand in it too, d-did you, Lucien?" Rodney's smile disbelieving, he raised his eyebrows in question.

Lucien glanced at Adam's warning expression. "So to speak, old chap. Only so to speak."

Adam breathed out a sigh of relief. "As soon as those plates are empty, I will see you both in the ballroom, matched up with ladies."

"Which lady d-do you want first, Lucien?" Toddington took an enormous bite of a meat pastry. A gentleman of limited means, he lived on his own in small digs in the city, with no facility for catering. As a consequence, he would eat any dish presented with equal gusto.

Lucien managed an off-hand expression. "I'll have the dark haired friend of Cornelia's, Miss Havers. Pretty little thing."

Toddington nodded. "She is more than pretty, but I think Jeremy has his eye on her as well."

Adam recalled to his mind Cornelia's dark-haired friend. If Jeremy were interested, the girl would be fast, no doubt. "Is George here yet?"

"Haven't seen him." Toddington took another careful bite. He had the manners of a gentleman and the appetite of a navvy. "I see you invited Mrs. Gates."

Adam suppressed a wince. "Not I. Cassia invited her. The two have become friends."

"That's rather inconvenient, old chap." Lucien's frown expressed his thoughts.

"We'll weather it, somehow." Adam rubbed the back of his neck. "The musicians are coming to the end of this bracket and in case neither of you listened, this is a supper dance, not merely a supper."

"I was racing through the first part, the supper, so that I would have plenty of time for the second," the shy Toddington said. "I've promised a d-dance to Miss Gerard."

Adam eyed the man. "Or has she promised one to you?"

"Ah, that's more gentlemanly, old chap. Please excuse my poor phrasing." Toddington used the smile that endeared him to most of London's women, young or old. He put his empty plate back on the table and wiped his hands on the napkin he had collected with the food. Then he drew a deep breath. "Back into the fray."

Lucien followed him into the dancing area. Adam stayed, making himself pleasant to the seated and gossiping chaperones, whom he knew from the times he had wandered into functions searching out Cassia. Since he had been married, none bothered him with hopeful introductions and instead treated him as another dupe who could help find partners for their charges. He duly noted that the count of chaperones had diminished, Cassia taking on the role as well, and using her cohort, Amelia Gates, to help her.

Perhaps his precious wife would like to forgive him for his mistake in criticizing her friend, and dance with him. For some nights, he hadn't had her in his arms. Although he didn't want to think that was her way of punishing him for being frank, he couldn't help but know. Last night, with a stormy expression on her normally calm face, she went to the trouble of whipping round to face him as he had tried to unhook her gown. Instead, she had called for her maid, Elsie, to help her disrobe.

Tonight he was determined to please his dear wife, since he certainly couldn't work with all these people in his house. Adopting a bland expression, he wandered back into the ballroom, where ladies and gentlemen galloped past in a long line before changing partners as the dance dictated. For a while, he propped up the wall.

Then George strolled into the room, greeting Adam with a wide smile. "Sorry to be late, Adam. I was working late. I had to read the bills of loading before tomorrow."

"The life of a worker isn't all it's cracked up to be, is it?" Adam gave the superior smile with which he expected to rile the other man.

George shook his head, not taking the bait. "No," he said dolefully. "It's work. A task quite distinct from idling. You know, much as I never thought I would say this, I am strangely enjoying it. To remain idle takes far more inventiveness."

Adam relaxed his shoulders and laughed. He turned to discover the presence looming behind him was his wife. Of course, since George had come, she *would* appear instantly. She greeted him with the sort of smile she hadn't shared with Adam for days. "George." She leaned forward to kiss him on the cheek, despite the fact that she had Amelia in tow. "You know my friend, Mrs. Gates, don't you?" She moved Amelia forward.

George managed a stiff bow. "I have had the pleasure. Mrs. Gates, how do you do?"

Mrs. Gates wore a splendid blue gown trimmed with silver braid. "I'm helping the duchess as a chaperone tonight, Mr. Penrose."

"I think everyone is taking a partner for a waltz," Cassia said to George, with expectation in her voice.

He raised his eyebrows. She nodded. He inclined his head toward Amelia. "Would you do me the honor of accepting me as your partner for this waltz, Mrs. Gates?"

Amelia widened her eyes at Cassia, and Cassia smiled at her friend. George took Amelia onto the floor.

"Neatly done," Adam said, drily. "As a chaperone, you excel."

"I thought so. I'm sure if, instead of disappearing, you had taken the initiative for the first dance and asked Amelia onto the floor, others would have followed. Failing you, who else but George would help me?"

He noted the criticism in her tone and lifted his eyebrows. "When you want me to leap to do your bidding, you must give me a hint, my dear."

"You are the host. You should set the tone." Her lips pressed together.

"What tone? Unrivalled licentiousness? Husbands dancing with ..." He saved himself before he said 'mistresses,' "... merry widows."

"Why not? As I said, you could have set an example. Amelia is too young to be left a widow and she is too lovely to be left unwed."

"If you think George will wed her, you are running up

the wrong alley." Growing more annoyed about Amelia by the second, Adam folded his arms across his chest.

"I have no one in particular in mind, but she will be shown to her best advantage while she is waltzing. Her husband was very respectable and now she has to work for a living. She is no less because of it." She raised her perfectly shaped chin high and tried to look down her nose at him, not easy when he was half a head taller than she.

He eyed her. Women who earned their way as mistresses didn't usually court respectability, but who was he to criticize? "May I show off my own dear bride on the dance floor?"

Her eyebrows lifted to match her chin. "If you can spare the time."

"Is that remark in some way significant?" He placed his arm on her waist and stood with her on the side of the room, awaiting the end of the country-dance.

"I shall not dwell on your neglect of me. I shall take this opportunity and enjoy dancing with you. I always did, you know."

Surprised into a smile, he studied her face. Tonight she looked particularly beautiful in an apricot silk gown. The color made her blue eyes a dazzling feature in her face. "Even when you were trying your hardest to evade me?"

"Even then. Now, be done with trying to eke compliments from me. You dance divinely and you know it." She melted into his arms.

His years of dancing lessons had paid off, although at sixteen he had despaired of the size of his feet. Fortunately, within the next year, the rest of him had grown to match, and he had learned to enjoy holding a woman in his arms. Now older, his adolescent fantasies no longer influenced his body's reactions. Dancing with a female no longer put a rod in his breeches. "Is tonight going as you planned?"

"The night has only just begun, and we have had no disasters as yet. The kitchen has managed rather well, though the maids will have a long night. I must make sure they have extra time off this week."

"And your matchmaking?"

"Matchmaking?"

"With George and Amelia."

She laughed. "He was the most convenient. Had he not been there, I would have accosted Lucien, though I must say, I think on an esoteric level that George and Amelia look well together."

"He's not a marrying man, Cassia."

"No one is a marrying man until he meets the right woman."

"Any woman will do for George," Adam muttered in a moment of exasperation, or possibly even jealousy. No matter what George did, in Cassia's eyes, he was perfect. Adam had no idea how to match him.

"Do you mean anything in particular by that, or are you casting aspersions on Amelia again?"

"No, not on Amelia."

"On George? Do you know something I should know?" Her gaze narrowed on his face.

"I know something you shouldn't know."

"That's a flag raiser, Adam. Now I will never rest until I know what you mean."

The music stopped, not only metaphorically. She stood

staring at his face, clearly trying to read his expression. Fortunately, the violinists began twiddling their musical thumbs in the break while the now idle guests began muffled conversations or moved toward the supper table. Lucien kept his dark-haired beauty's hand on his arm while he escorted her to supper. Adam glanced away from the couple, back to his wife, and he sighed. "I'm bound to tell you sooner or later, but I doubt this is the place."

"You must be the most irritating man in the whole world, Adam. You make a leading statement at an inappropriate time and then you expect me to wait to find out what you mean."

"Never mind. You can drop the subject because I have decided not to tell you after all." He folded his arms across his chest.

She stared at him, bared her teeth, swung around, and left him standing alone.

"And that, my lad, is what you get for marrying in haste," he rumbled to himself as he sought out Jeremy in the supper room.

Cassia called for Elsie to help her undress. Her apricot gown was put away, and she had already donned her red silk robe, a recent gift from Adam, when the man himself strode into her dressing room. She offered him a placating smile. He had been so supportive tonight that she was proud to be his wife. At all times, he had acted like the gentleman he was and no young lady had been left without a partner. With luck, this year's debutants would not remain long on the shelf. "That went off well. Were you pleased with the event?"

"It's not quite the same to host a supper dance as it is to attend one. I hadn't realized I would be so busy talking to all and sundry."

"As a bachelor, you held up the walls with your back. As a married man, you have to be a responsible citizen."

"I have discovered that. I can say that being the host of a social function is no different from presiding over a meeting. I simply needed to have the right people in the vicinity of each other, and conversations ensued."

She laughed. "Jeremy seemed to enjoy himself. He is quite a flirt. Poor Lucien. He is so rigid. He didn't have a chance with Miss Havers when Jeremy was around. I suspect she will find a husband in no time. Essie and Bertie already seem to be a couple."

"Bertie has had his eye on Essie for years. I think he has made a good match. As for Miss Havers ..."

"You don't think Jeremy is serious?"

"I have no idea. She is incredibly beautiful but I don't think she has two thoughts to knock together. She certainly couldn't manage a conversation with me."

"Perhaps she is a little shy. I had no problem with her. As for her looks, yes, she is stunning."

He shrugged. "Are you tired?"

"In a wonderful way. I absolutely loved tonight. I think I must be more managing than I realized. I do like organizing functions and I love putting people together."

"How strange you should mention the latter, my precious. I love putting people together too, namely you and me, in bed. You must be tired."

"Oh, I'm enormously tired. I think I shall go straight to sleep." Her expression deliberately innocent, she eyed him as she left the dressing room. Any woman would know what he had on his mind, and she thought he might have suffered enough. Should he approach her in bed, she wouldn't push him away. Aside from that, she had already begun to tingle below for need of his expert tending.

As she walked past the foot of the bed, he grabbed the tie of her dressing robe, which dropped to the floor. Without wasting a second, he tugged her sleeve. She spun around, her outer garment sliding onto the floral patterned carpet. His arms encircled her, and he covered her lips with his. Naturally, she buried her finger in his thick dark hair and pasted her body to his. With a quick lift, he had her on the bed with himself covering her.

"My beautiful Cassia," he said, his breath hot against her throat. "You've had me on rations and now you must pay."

"My beautiful Adam. You've kept secrets from me, and now you must reveal all." She pushed his hair back from his face and stared into his smoldering eyes.

He shook his head. "Not now, my love. I have urgent business first." His mouth dipped into a smile as he took her buttocks into his competent hands. One kiss, and she writhed against him. The man was impossible, but he had skills and a mouth she could not resist.

Finally after he had pleasured her and himself, he lay beside her, his arms still around her. The orange light of dawn gave his skin a golden appearance. Her head rested on his chest. His heart pounded against her ear and she toyed with the hair on his chest, a dark cover that spread from one side of his upper rib cage to the other before making a downy track to his navel and beyond. Her palm followed the track to beyond, only to find he had begun to thicken again.

"What do you know about George that I don't?" she said in a husky whisper, not sure if she honestly cared.

"He is not quite as perfect as you suppose," he said after drawing in a deep breath. He watched her hand.

She huffed a soft laugh onto his chest. "I don't imagine anyone is quite as perfect as I suppose. Sooner or later I will come to the same conclusion about you."

"Would you like to expand on my perfections first?" His breath stirred her hair and his hand tightened around her waist.

"Would you like to expand on George's imperfections *first*?"

He emptied his chest with a deep sigh. "Do you know why his father called him back to Surrey before we married?"

"I assumed he wanted to offer him the job he now has."

"He was due a reprimand. His baby was about to be born and he had forgotten to leave his lover with enough money to look after herself."

"You are not serious!"

"The girl was a maid in his father's house. The housekeeper dismissed her when she started growing a belly."

"That is monstrous." Shocked to her core, Cassia pushed herself up and stared into Adam's eyes. "Surely not."

"He gave her a handful of money so that her mother would take her back while she had the child." He sighed deeply. "When the money ran out, her mother went to Mr. Penrose. She thought that was not good enough. As it happens, nor did Mr. Penrose. Bastard or not, he wanted to know his grandson."

"It was a boy?"

"With hair as fair as his father."

Cassia lay on her back, thinking. Perhaps she should have been disgusted by this news but she had always known that George was a little unsteady. "I didn't know George was so irresponsible." Perhaps that was why she had never made a solid plan with him in her life. She had said to herself that if all else failed, she would marry him, but she wondered that if push came to shove if she would ever have done so. He needed a wife but a less exacting one than she, who would want to love him and encourage him onto the right track. He had no bad in him; no evil. He simply didn't have any great ambitions.

"It could happen to anyone. Not everyone gets caught." Adam smoothed his thumb along her jaw line, a comforting gesture she appreciated.

"You would support a by-blow, surely, Huntsdale?"

"I would, but I don't have one. I didn't ever need to chase after housemaids."

She stared at the ornate ceiling rose, gathering her thoughts together. Instead of chasing housemaids, Adam had taken a mistress, who clearly trained him well in the art of lovemaking. For that, Cassia should be grateful, at least. "Jeremy does. Perhaps you need to give him a little talk."

"I'll think it over. The way he normally responds to my little talks is to go exactly where he was headed, but faster." He lifted Cassia on top of him and what with one thing and another, she decided Jeremy wasn't the first of her considerations at this time.

During the morning, she occupied herself getting the house back in order, though she congratulated herself on the success of her first supper dance. All the young ladies had enjoyed themselves in the more casual setting than the grand balls that they had attended this season. Cassia noted a few promising relationships. Essie was certain to receive an offer from Bertie. Perhaps Cornelia wasn't so certain to receive one from Jeremy. Her friend, Miss Havers, seemed to have caught his attention instead. As for Lucien, he also appeared smitten by the quiet young lady, too. Perhaps Cassia could hint Lucien onto Amelia, because George was now out of the running. She couldn't encourage her friend to think of a man who was so unsteady, despite that fact that Amelia had pink cheeks and a smile the whole time she had danced with him.

The rest of Cassia's day disappeared in incidentals, like delivering food to the boys' home. Boys always needed food. Sunday was taken up by the cricket match. On Monday, she dropped by to see Amelia. "Please, wait," Cassia said to her coachman, not certain if Amelia would be at home, or how busy she might be.

The door opened. Amelia looked surprised to see Cassia. "Oh, do come in. I have just arrived home. I have been with Miss Deering, advising her on her gowns. She is wanting to make sure of a proposal."

"I wish her good luck. I have come for nothing more productive than a gossip—a review of my supper dance."

"I had a lovely time, Cassia." A soft smile on her face,

Amelia showed her into the sitting room. "I wasn't expecting to be asked to dance. I hope you don't mind."

"Oh, dear. I truly wished you had stayed on the sidelines while I and everyone else danced, but what could I do when you were so popular with the gentlemen?" Cassia laughed. "Silly. Of course I wanted you to enjoy yourself."

"I did. Tremendously. Did you like Cornelia Gerard's gown?"

"Very pretty. Were you the one who advised her mother to replace those huge frills around the neckline?"

"I did. Such a petite young lady is easily lost behind large trimmings. I couldn't help but notice that your brother-in-law treats her more like a sister than she would like."

"The two families have known each other forever. That's to be expected."

"But disappointing for her nonetheless."

"We can't match-make for everyone. What did you think about Lucien Walton?"

"He seems rather nice."

"Rather specially nice?"

Amelia shrugged. "He seemed to have his eye on Miss Havers. In fact, most of the young men did."

"Let's hope she marries soon so that the other young ladies have a chance. I know you liked my friend, George Penrose, but I must warn you about him."

Amelia's eyes focused on Cassia's. "What do you mean?"

"I don't think he would be right for you. He isn't entirely honorable. I still like him, but he is a trifle unsteady and loose with his morals. Not that it couldn't happen to anyone, Adam says, but if it happened to Adam, I would be very disappointed in him. I want to think he would be more responsible."

"What happened to Mr. Penrose?" Amelia held her gaze.

"All the gentlemen know, but not the young ladies. I can tell you, but I hope you won't share my information with the others."

"I am certain not to," Amelia said in a dry tone. "I'm not on gossiping terms with the younger ladies. I advise them about their wardrobe and their hair, but nothing else. I hear a few confidences, but I don't gossip."

"When he went back to Surrey, he had been called back by his father because a maid had his baby. He left her without support and he had to explain himself."

Amelia stared at her hands. "And did he offer to marry her?"

Cassia shook her head. "I am sure his father would have been furious if George wanted to marry a servant. But he made sure George supported her and the child. That's why George had to begin working—to earn his way out of the mess."

Amelia offered a crooked smile. "I'm sure he is sorry. As the duke said, it could happen to anyone."

"It disappointed me, though. Still, I don't have the right to hold high standards for anyone but myself, and even I don't live up to my own hopes."

"Oh, Cassia, you are as close to perfect as any woman can be."

Cassia shook her head, laughing. "I'm righteous and unforgiving. Look at how long it took for me to see Adam as a gentleman. I thought, because he had a mistress, that he was irredeemable, but he isn't. I'm growing quite attached to him, I swear."

"Aren't you in love with him, Cassia?" Amelia's eyes widened.

"What would be the point? I would have to moon around after him all the time, and he would hate that. I would have to bring 'the duke says' into every conversation, and then I would bore everyone to death. This way, I can do all that he needs a wife to do."

She thought about those words that night in bed. Her father had taught her that wives were meant to see to the comfort of their husbands, to help them succeed in their endeavors, and to bear children. She had only seen to Adam's comfort where she wanted the comfort to be, in his home, with his meals, and when she wanted, in his bed. She laughed a little laugh.

Mainly, she had seen to her comfort foremost, and if her comfort worked for him as well, that was all to the good. Was she dutiful? If it suited her. In fact, she had pleased herself in every aspect of her marriage, and Adam hadn't objected one bit. Perhaps wives were as much companions as born and bred comforters.

At times, she had wondered if she wasn't a little more than attached to him. She hoped not. That wouldn't do. A man who hadn't hesitated to take a mistress soon after he reached his majority would expect to marry comfortably and not bother about the other aspects of being part of a couple. He knew he could find the pleasures of the flesh elsewhere. But, of course, if she discovered that he did, he would be left with his 'elsewhere woman.' His wife would simply be a wife in name. At this stage, he seemed to be enjoying her, and she certainly enjoyed him. When she palled on him, if she didn't love him, she wouldn't be heartbroken. Then she wouldn't mind at all.

She snuggled into his big, warm body. In his sleep, he gathered her up with one arm, resting his cheek on her hair. At moments like these, she was perfectly content.

Chapter Thirteen

Mellie's maid opened the door to Huntsdale and showed him into the sitting room. "The mistress will be with you in a moment." He sat on the chaise longue, tapping the brim of his hat on his knee.

Mellie rustled into the room soon after, a puzzled smile on her face. "Huntsdale, my dear. Should you be here at this time of the day?" Her fingers toyed with a ribbon trimming on her sleeve.

He shrugged. "I doubt my wife has anyone spying on your house."

"Nevertheless, you know how people talk." Resuming her nonchalant expression, she arranged herself gracefully on the armless chair, her skirts spread around her. As usual, she wore a beautifully-made gown in a shade of blue that flattered her. She stared directly into his eyes. "How long have I known you?"

He kept her gaze. "Two years."

"Which means I know you well enough to realize that

you wouldn't openly drop by for a chat. If something is bothering you, please tell me, my dear."

"I thought we could simply chat, and my mind would be eased, and I would find …" He dragged in a breath.

"Find what?" She sighed. "Will offering you a glass of brandy loosen up your tongue?"

"Did it ever?" He managed a half smile.

She shook her head. "Well, then, let us begin with a nice chat about the weather."

He curled his mouth cynically. "The current weather is exactly what is needed for my crops to grow. The current weather is making my wife happy because she is preparing the garden for who knows what." He drew in a deep breath. "The current weather makes no difference at all to me when my life is out of kilter." As the words left his lips, he wished them unsaid. A self-contained man, he had never accepted that he needed to confide in another. To finally admit to himself that he didn't have Cassia's love revealed to him a truth that he could no longer ignore. He wanted Cassia for reasons other than her suitability. He loved her mind as much as he loved her body. Without the one, the other seemed meaningless.

Mellie's eyes changed to a murky, unreadable color. "I hope we are not about to have the misunderstood husband conversation, because I thought better of you."

He glanced away, wishing he hadn't come. "I am not here to discuss my wife."

"If you are not here to ask me to have you back … you are asking, I think, for my help."

"Advise, perhaps. Do you see me as inadequate?"

Her mouth curved ruefully. "As a man? No, my dear. If

you are fishing for compliments, I can say quite honestly that I much enjoyed your lovemaking. If I hadn't, I wouldn't have stayed with you."

"Aside from that," he asked impatiently.

She narrowed her eyes as if considering. "When you bother to try, your conversation is intelligent and interesting. Even without your fortune, any woman with a modicum of sense would find you highly attractive."

He clamped his jaw.

"Have I answered your questions?"

"What would you do if you found out I had lied to you?" He avoided her gaze.

For a moment she remained silent. "But surely you have no need to?"

"No one has a need to lie, but sometimes a person is forced into it."

"Was yours a convenient lie or a lie to protect another?"

He turned his signet ring a full circle, watching, while he tried to select his words. "Both," he said, slowly. "An omission of the truth, rather than a lie."

She spread her hands. "Even if I presume the person you kept the truth from is not me, I can't possibly answer your question, Adam. All of us do one or the other at times. I am not going to guess whom you kept a certain truth from, but ask yourself if you were in the other's situation, would you rather have heard the truth or would you have preferred the omission? Now, I don't know if I have helped or not, but you really must leave. If your carriage is seen outside, people will gossip. Now that I am making a new life for myself, I do not need this any more than you do."

As Adam travelled back home through the busy street,

he pondered telling Cassia that she had been deliberately locked in the shed with him because he had said he wanted time alone with her. The locking had been no accident at all.

He had the chance in bed that night, but she seemed to be in an adventurous mood. She had decided to straddle him and investigate his body, which somewhat distracted him, especially when she concentrated on his lower body. Tonight, she had decided to experiment with his foreskin. Although he kept trying to grow out of it, she kept making it fit. "Fascinating," she said, almost sounding clinical until she laughed. "I think if I had one of these, I would fiddle with it constantly, as little boys do."

"Big boys do, too." His voice came out huskier than usual. He'd had no idea when he had married her, that relations between them would be so much better than anything he'd previously experienced. "You might try putting your new toy elsewhere."

"Whatever could you possibly be hinting?"

"That you may be able to enjoy me as much as I enjoy you." He could have spoken then. He could have said that he loved her, but the words sat in his heart, unexpressed. The risk of changing a playful moment into an awkward situation was not one he could manage at this point. She leaned down to kiss him. For a while he could concentrate only on her mouth but her toy began to nudge at her and what with one thing and another, she ended up beneath him, breathing hard, and importuning him. When he had worn himself out pleasuring her, he snuggled her into him. Her head fit neatly beneath his chin. Now would be the time to whisper words of love. With idle fingers, he began to stroke her hair.

She pressed her face into his bare skin. Her breaths dragged slowly in and out. Her hand completely relaxed on his shoulder.

He dropped a kiss on the top of her head. "Are you asleep?"

"Mm."

He already knew that she disliked being disturbed. Or perhaps he wasn't the lover he thought he was, and she'd had enough of him tonight.

Perhaps tonight wasn't the time to try to whisper words of love.

Instead, he closed his eyes, savored the scent of her hair, and held her until he, too, slept.

Cassia had managed to gather together a sewing circle, comprising Lady Gerard, Cornelia Gerard, Mrs. Deering and her daughter Essie, and Amelia. Cassia hoped to expand the group but since she had only been gathering helpers for a few weeks, she thought she had been quite successful. Lady Gerard had cut out the tiny gowns and the others would sew the pieces together while discussing recipes or anyone worthy of gossip.

George Penrose was the first to occupy the mind of the ladies. "Now that he is living in town, we ought to be matchmaking for him. What do you think of my friend,

Miss Havers, for him?" Cornelia finished a tiny hem with a flourish.

Essie smiled. "She is very beautiful. I think Jeremy Everley wants her, too."

"I could stare at Rodney Toddington all day," Cornelia said, surprisingly. "If we are discussing men who are easy on the eye."

A sigh issued from the lungs of six ladies, young and older.

"You would think Rodney had everything a man could wish for, but I believe he has a broken heart." Lady Gerard reached for a new thread. "Time will heal all, I expect."

"I always thought Huntsdale would be a hardened old bachelor, and now look. He's the first to be married. I expect Bertie will be next." Cornelia glanced at Essie, who managed to appear unaware, although her cheeks tinged with pink.

"I wonder who Lord Walton will choose. He seems very taken with Miss Havers, too, Cornelia. We must invite her to stay with us in Surrey. We should be leaving in another month."

Cornelia nodded at her mother. "She may like to join the sewing circle, too. I will ask her. She was very handy with a needle at school."

Cassia's eyes met Amelia's. Tales of school days didn't include either of them, since Cassia had been educated at home, and Amelia clearly hadn't attended their exclusive school. When the ladies, or even the gentlemen, started the *who knows whom, from where* conversations, outsiders like Cassia and Amelia had little to do but nod.

"Please ask her, Cornelia." Cassia inspected the little

gown on her lap. A cross stitch would help the neckline to sit properly. She would like to add lace, but the amount of gowns interested Sister Frederica at the babies' home more than the detailing. "We can't have too many ladies helping us."

Cornelia lifted her gaze. "She has a sister, too, if you want me to include her in the invitation?"

"The more the merrier." Cassia passed the scissors to Lady Gerard who appeared to be searching for a pair.

"Now we have Lucien sorted, we should think of Jeremy," Lady Gerard said rather mischievously. She knew Cornelia had an interest in Cassia's brother-in-law. Everyone knew except Jeremy, who saw every member of the Gerard family as quite wonderful, since they had accepted him into their home after his parents died, Adam being at Oxford at the time.

"Mama! You know very well that Jeremy is too young to be thinking of marriage." Her daughter aimed a quelling grimace at her parent.

"In that case, I'll have to match-make for George instead."

"I suspect, given a chance, he would make a young lady a very good husband," Amelia said quietly. "Like the other young gentlemen I met at Cassia's supper dance. Each one of them made sure I was not left without a partner, which was very generous, considering I am not a young lady making her debut."

Cassia smiled at her friend, puzzled that she hadn't expected attention from the gentlemen. "Not so generous, Amelia. You are a beautiful woman, and they lined up to dance with you. My, Cornelia, your backstitch is perfect. I do believe we'll have another five gowns ready today. Sister Frederica will be so thrilled. I'll be able to have them packaged up and sent off tomorrow."

"Next time, could I take home a few we have finished?" Cornelia bit off a thread. "My sister, Daisy, would never apply herself to sewing, but she embroiders sweet little roses when the mood takes her. I'm sure little baby girls would love to have decorated nightgowns."

"I'm sure they would too, Cornelia. Even if they don't notice, their mothers will. Take home the gowns we made today and we'll end up with a bigger bundle next week. And please thank your sister."

Dora, the parlor maid, arrived with tea and macaroons, which Amelia waved away. Lately she had avoided sweets. Cassia wondered if she had a touch of the nasty cold that had passed through the city during the recent winter. As Cassia dropped her off that afternoon, she invited Amelia to an informal dinner with Adam and Jeremy the next night. Amelia pleaded another engagement. With Cassia an idle wife and Amelia a working-woman, times together were difficult to arrange. Not having an excuse to lure Amelia out of the house, she had to wait another week to see her friend.

When she went to pick up Amelia for the next sewing bee, Amelia didn't come to the door herself. "Mrs. Gates will be with you soon," her housemaid said importantly. "She's had a touch of queasiness. Always gets it in the morning," she added as if she had imparted useful information, and left Cassia waiting in the sitting room.

Within a few minutes, Amelia stood in the doorway, pushing a hatpin into the lovely flower creation she wore in her auburn curls. "So sorry to hold you up. I hope my maid gave my apologies."

"She said you are always queasy in the mornings. Have you seen a doctor?"

Amelia nodded. "I should be quite well soon, he said. The queasiness is expected to pass."

Cassia nodded, though how a doctor would know that, she couldn't imagine. However, he turned out to be right. When Cassia delivered her back home the next week, Amelia turned to her before leaving the carriage. "I'm sorry, Cassia, but this must be the last time I join your sewing circle."

Cassia took her hands. "I'm a wretch, taking up all your time with my own projects. I have so appreciated your help with the nightwear, Amelia, but I quite understand. I'll visit you rather than carrying you off once a week."

Amelia dropped her gaze. "Best you don't, Cassia. I will be far too busy."

"Far too busy for me to visit you?"

"I'm afraid so. You are a duchess and I have a wage to earn. Don't think I'm not grateful for all the customers you have thrown my way. I am."

"You don't *honestly* think our current differences in station means we can't be friends?" Cassia asked, trying not to be offended. She had never thought of herself above anyone because of her new title, which she had gained by being trapped in a shed overnight with Adam. He would have married any woman whom he had compromised, because he was a man of honor.

"I do, Cassia. Your sewing group is very kind to me, but

I can't keep taking advantage of your patronage. I'm not a suitable friend for you, Cassia, and I must say goodbye."

"I can't see why you are not suitable." Cassia knew her voice sounded mulish. "We have everything in common. We love the same plays, we read the same books, we laugh at the same jokes. You are kinder than I am, and you are the very sort of person I should be influenced by."

"I'm sure the duke doesn't share your views on me." Amelia averted her gaze.

"My husband doesn't choose my friends."

"I'm right, aren't I?"

Cassia's cheeks warmed. "He has never said anything against you. I wouldn't listen if he did."

"Soon everyone will be gossiping about me. I would rather drop the people I like before they are forced to ignore me."

"Why would anyone be forced to ignore you? What has happened?"

"I'm about to ... perhaps I should move to the country." Amelia wrung her hands together. "Then I can't embarrass you."

Cassia snatched her friend's hands into hers. "Amelia, please trust me."

Amelia wiped her tongue over her bottom lip. "This house ... I don't pay for the upkeep. Do you understand? Cassia, I'm not a respectable woman."

Cassia swallowed. "You're saying that a man supports you? Would he be the same one who owns the carriage you borrowed?" She knew the brand well, and she knew none but the wealthy could own one. Amelia's man could even be someone from her social circle.

Amelia nodded. "He is very generous to me," she said quietly, her gaze averted. "I'm not saying any of your sewing circle suspects me, because I don't think they would lower themselves to speak with me if so, but soon everyone will know I am a fallen woman."

Cassia clutched Amelia's hands. She couldn't approve of Amelia being a mistress, and without a doubt society would cut her if they knew. Suffering the same fate herself because of befriending Amelia would be unlikely, but that wouldn't help her friend. "You don't need to rely on this man for support. You could come and live with us. We have eight bedrooms and plenty of room. It would be no trouble—"

"Don't you understand, Duchess. I'm with child. I will be producing a baby in a little under six months."

Cassia breathed out. "Oh, dear. This does complicate matters. Does the father plan to marry you?"

Amelia shook her head. Her eyes glossed with unshed tears, and she turned, removing her hands from Cassia's light hold. "He doesn't know about the baby." She opened the carriage door and took one step down.

"May I come inside with you to discuss this?" Helpless, Cassia stood, her mind whirling with plans, none useful, none at this stage worthy of being presented.

Amelia turned, her face pale. "Please don't. You are only making this harder."

Cassia blinked and sat again. "I can't leave you like this."

"I'm the one who got myself into this mess and I have to accept the consequences."

"Will he support you?"

"I hope so. He did say he loved me, but I believe I may not be the only woman who has heard those words from him. Thank you for taking this so well, my dear friend." Amelia avoided eye contact as she closed the door firmly on Cassia.

The carriage drove off. Cassia had no intention of heeding Amelia's words. Nothing could force her to drop a woman who so desperately needed a friend. She would have to sit and decide what she ought to do.

If Amelia's lover wouldn't take responsibility for his actions, Amelia would be in dire straits. If he did, Amelia would still be left unmarried and disgraced. She was already known as a widow, therefore using that ploy wouldn't work again unless Cassia fabricated such a complicated story about him not dying until recently that she would be certain to trip herself up.

After dinner that night, she read a book instead of sewing. If she sewed, she would concentrate on her stitches, whereas with a book in her lap, she could appear to be reading instead of thinking. Every plan she pondered had a vital flaw. The man involved was certainly disreputable, having an affair with a woman when he knew he wouldn't marry her if anything of an untoward nature occurred.

When Adam joined her in bed, she watched him fuss with his pillow and said, "What would you do if you had given your mistress a baby?"

He stared at her, his expression cautious. "I didn't."

"That's not a proper answer."

"That wasn't a proper question. A man doesn't impregnate his mistress. Mistresses have a way of avoiding that event."

"How do they avoid it?"

He breathed out. "Has no woman discussed this with you?"

"Who would? I don't imagine my mother knew, but I wasn't of an age to be told anyway by the time she died."

He lay flat on his back, drawing his dark eyebrows together, apparently as an aid for inspiration. "Well, there's, ah, a method like a cap or a sponge chemically treated. A man can always, ah, remove himself in time, or he can wear protection." He evaded her gaze.

"What did you do when you were with your mistress?"

His eyebrows moved to a lower position. "Wives don't ask these things."

"Wives need to know as much as mistresses, surely?" She tried not to concentrate on his wide, muscular chest, for she was determined not to be sidetracked by his wondrous body yet again.

His fingers threaded together across his tight belly and he stared in that direction, clearly unwilling to meet her gaze. "The last two. I'm sure my mistress did the first, but we never discussed the matter other than to agree that ours was a strictly formal arrangement."

"It doesn't sound too formal to me." She sat up, leaning her back against the headboard, crossing her arms. "What do you do to make sure I don't have a baby?"

"You're my wife. I ..." He cleared his throat. "I hope to have babies with you," he finished in a stiff voice.

"What do you think about a man who gets his mistress with child?"

"You mean George?"

"Of course not. I mean someone who gives a baby to a respectable woman."

"Don't you think the housemaid he impregnated was a respectable woman?"

"I don't know," she said irritably. "I'm not trying to judge women. I'm trying to work out what sort of man would leave a woman high and dry when she is carrying his child."

"I think you have answered your own question. If a man loved a woman, he would not do that to her. Now, is this conversation over?"

She slid back down again. "Apparently." Rolling over, she faced away from him. Losing a friend because of the inconsiderate behavior of a man hurt. At this moment, she didn't feel in charity with any male, least of all her husband, who'd had a close relationship with a woman other than his wife. Hm. So had George. Well, she didn't care what George did. She needed to sleep. She could barely keep her eyes open now, anyway.

In the morning she awoke tangled in the sheets and grumpy. Adam had left. She struggled out of bed, entirely focused on Amelia. She would not be told who to keep as a friend, be it the friend or not. Adam had finished his breakfast and gone out by the time she went down for a meal. Jeremy ambled into the dining room before she had finished her plate of stewed fruit. "Good morning, Jeremy."

"Good morning, Cassia. Did you leave any scrambled eggs for me?"

"In the warmer. That's if Adam didn't eat them all. I don't know what time he left."

"There's a swag here. I expect the toast is soggy, though."

"If it is, ring. Someone will make more."

"You look tired," he said, sitting with his soggy toast and his solid egg mass. "Were you out until the small hours?"

She had noticed before that he wasn't at all particular about his food, other than the incredible amount he managed to consume daily. "That gives me an estimate of the time you came in, if you don't know that we were in bed long before. Adam likes to arise early, and he isn't enthusiastic about late nights."

"Not these days, no. He has changed since he married you. He used to work late, that is, on the nights when he didn't visit ... by high-water, these eggs are tough."

"If they've been sitting in the warmer for an hour, they are bound to be." Cassia didn't miss the reference to Adam visiting, which would have ended with the name of his mistress. He was as bad as Amelia's man. Adam hadn't minded availing himself of the woman, but he had married Cassia. "Do you have a mistress, Jeremy?" She could count her brother-in-law out as the father of Amelia's baby. He didn't have a sneaky bone in his entire body. His life was an open book.

Jeremy shook his head. "Not yet."

"Do you expect to take one?"

"Everyone does." He stuffed his mouth full of eggs and toast.

"Everyone?"

"Almost everyone," he amended, his fork searching out another huge mouthful. "You can be sure Bertie won't. Nor would Lucien. Stands to reason they can't when they were so critical of ... oh, hell. You've got me talking too early in the morning when my tongue is still loose from the wine the night before."

"I know Adam had a mistress, Jeremy. Everyone does. Know. And George had that woman in the country. I suppose that counts."

"Ha."

"What do you mean by *ha*?"

"I know he is a friend of yours, Cassia, but George is certainly no saint."

"As I discovered when I heard about his housemaid in Surrey." Cassia leaned back, pushing the stewed apples aside. She reached for a slice of cold, soggy toast.

"He doesn't confine his activities to Surrey, and I will say no more on that subject."

"Nor should you. I shouldn't know about these things. Wives don't."

He glanced at her. "Has someone been gossiping to you? I'm sure there was nothing in it, Cassia. Adam wouldn't take up with Mellie again, not now he is married to you."

Cassia's chest froze. *Wouldn't take up with Mellie again? Mellie?* She swallowed her fear, deciding she would not ask why Jeremy had made that comment. Instead, she offered him a tight smile. "Everyone gossips. You should know that."

"And you women most of all."

She let that statement alone, rather than be outraged. None of the women she knew spread juicy gossip about others. They simply talked about events and gave opinions about people.

The whole of the day she did nothing but ruminate about *nothing being in it* and Adam probably not taking up his mistress again, until finally coming to the unbearable conclusion that Adam had been spotted with Mellie. People, meaning men, had discussed the matter and had decided to let Adam pass muster. She rubbed the back of her neck to ease her tension, trying to work on her useful thoughts rather than her dreadful thoughts.

Whether his meeting with the woman had been accidental or not, Cassia would be a fool not to take note. She would be bigger fool to ask him. In her experience of accusing her half brothers, both took the default position to lie. She placed her palms on her hot cheeks in an attempt to cool the heating caused by panicking.

Her instinct was to trust him. After all, as far as she knew, he had never lied to her, and he had always treated her with respect. He had proposed to her after they had been caught in a compromising position. The points in his favor finally convinced her that there *was* probably nothing in it.

Jeremy being out that night, she and Adam ate dinner early, having been invited to attend a card evening later. "You left early this morning," Cassia said politely.

"You were not pleased with me the night before. I wanted to give you time to, ah ..."

"Think better of questioning you about your mistress?"

"I doubt that's what you were doing. You wanted to know how to prevent a baby. If you are not ready, I will be more careful in the future." His voice sounded stiff.

Annoyed that he misread her and that husbands, or men in general, appeared not to discuss this choice, she stared at him with her chin lifted. "That is extremely considerate of you," she said smoothly, "but I think the best thing to do is to have separate rooms."

He crashed his fist on the table. The cutlery leapt high, dropped, and shivered back into place. "Do not imagine, wife, that you are so irresistible that I cannot sleep beside you without touching you." Having dealt speedily with her insurrection, he lifted his wineglass, quaffed the remains, scraped back his chair, and left the room.

She sat staring at the slammed door.

Dora came creeping into the room. "Should I take the plates, your grace?" she whispered.

Cassia smiled at the timid maid. "I think we can safely say that dinner is over. Thank you, Dora."

The card party became a non-event. Adam left the house. Cassia sat alone, sewing. After she had retired, very much later that night, Adam thumped into bed beside her, smelling like a tavern. She had no idea what prompted her to say that she would like separate rooms. Later tomorrow, Nora and Papa would be arriving with the boys for a few days. Her marriage would appear most unfortunate if she and her husband had decided to sleep apart.

She dropped by to see Amelia the next day. Fortunately, she wasn't refused admittance. "I have finally tested Adam to the limit," she said, as Amelia led her to the sitting room. "He lost his temper with me."

"Oh, Cassia. Don't take on so. He loves you. All will be well."

"Of course he doesn't love me. In fact, I'm almost sure

he has begun to see his mistress again. I shouldn't mind, but I do. Anyway, that's not why I came. You must remember that my family will be arriving from Surrey today and that I am holding my spring party on Saturday night. I can't manage alone, Amelia."

"Of course you can. You are the most competent lady of my acquaintance. You've managed large events for years, or so you told me."

"I have, but they were in the country and not at all formal. I wasn't a duchess then and I do need a friend to help me, Amelia. And you promised you would attend. It would look very strange if you suddenly weren't there. What would I say to people?"

Amelia narrowed her eyes to scrutinize the expression on Cassia's. "I'm sure no one will ask."

"It will be a miserable function with Adam stalking around furious and me huddled in misery."

Amelia laughed. "I've never known anyone quite as unscrupulous as you, Duchess. Your over-exaggeration is masterful. If you hadn't made me smile, I am sure I would cry for you."

"So you will help me?" Cassia leaned forward and grasped Amelia's hands.

"For the last time. Then I really must make arrangements to leave before I begin to show."

"Amelia, my dearest friend. I'm sure we will muddle through this somehow. I'm just not sure how, yet. But trust me. I will think of something."

Chapter Fourteen

With his wife's relatives underfoot, Adam remained scrupulously polite to his recalcitrant wife. Fortunately, he could disappear to his study on the first day. On the second day, the house was awash with women and flowers. Not only was Lady Lacey underfoot, Amelia appeared to live in his house, too. Cassia's two young stepbrothers played a game that consisted of skidding in their stockings across the marble tiles in the front hall. The game ended when one cannoned into the hall table. This took Lady Lacey out of the action for a while, nursing his bleeding nose.

Throughout all the noise and fuss, the cursed woman he had married sailed through with apparently not a care in the world. Assuredly, she spent a fortune. At least ten maids chatted in the halls, leaving a man with work to do no peace. "I think we ought to go to Whites," he said to his father-in-law, who looked as helpless as Adam.

"Good idea. If I don't disappear soon, I will be asked to take the boys to see the balloon ascension or some other thing sure to exhaust me. I must keep up my energy for tonight, when I will be expected to do heaven knows what."

"I'm not sure what Cassia is planning, but since we have musicians setting up, it's bound to be noisy," Adam said resignedly.

"You don't know what Cassia is planning? Good Lord, man. You surely didn't let her have her head?"

Adam stared at Sir Robert. "I imagined she didn't need my input."

"She doesn't need input. She needs a limit set as to the budget."

Since Adam's budget had no limit, he saw no point in changing the situation. As a matter of fact, the one asset he wanted in a wife was organizational skills. Well, the other assets were strong mindedness, intelligent conversation, a sense of humor, an independent mind, and apparently long, thick, pale hair. The fact that she also excelled in bedroom sports almost seemed incidental.

The fact that she had banned this last had his mind scurrying as to how to change the situation, short of apologizing for something he hadn't done. Something he wouldn't do—be unfaithful to the only woman he wanted. However, he certainly wouldn't grovel to a woman, not even the one he loved. "Too late. It's done. And now we should leave them to it."

Although he and Sir Robert shared a smooth old wine at the club, Adam was still unable to relax. He left a few hours later in good time to dress for what the servants now seemed to be calling a spring party. The day had been cool, but not cold. As he and Sir Robert walked through the hall, a footman staggered under a tray of glasses, heading for the ballroom. The new parlor maid, Dora, followed him carrying a large amount of napery.

"Back just in time, I see," Sir Robert said, sounding pleased. "Any later and I would have my head handed to me."

"I'm sure we have an hour."

Sir Robert eyed him. "Your guests have an hour. Husbands have ten minutes because they need to look at everything and make no comment other than to praise the wife's efforts. Then, of course, he must praise the wife's appearance."

"I had no idea husbands had a set of rules. Are there any others?"

Sir Robert laughed. "Dance with the senior ladies first, make sure the gentlemen have drinks, and kindly dispose of those who have taken too many. That should cover your night."

Adam nodded, humoring him, and strode upstairs to change. His valet had his evening clothes prepared. When outfitted to the man's satisfaction, Adam knocked on the door of his wife's dressing room. He heard female voices. "Are you ready?" he asked in a low voice.

"I want to wear the green, but Elsie wants me to wear the yellow. What do you think?"

He opened the door. "I'll need to see a sample before I can give my opinion."

Elsie looked scandalized, and she quickly threw a dressing robe over Cassia's bare shoulders. He offered her a reproving glance. "My wife is covered, Elsie. No need to be embarrassed for her."

Cassia took no notice. "This is what I want to wear, the

green silk I wore for my wedding. Amelia assured me it suits me. This is the yellow satin Elsie wants me to wear."

"Either would suit you. However, the yellow would look better with the diamond choker."

"What diamond choker?" She eyed him warily.

"This one." He drew the piece consisting of three rows of small diamonds surrounding a larger one set in the front, out of his pocket. The trinket had been ordered after their sparse honeymoon and had been delivered today.

"What do you think, Elsie?" Cassia studied the choker, frowning. "Should I wear the diamonds for a supper party or would I look overdressed?"

"I'm sure I don't know, ma'am. If I had a necklace like that, I would wear it under my uniform. I wouldn't let it out of my sight."

"In that case, I shall wear the yellow."

She didn't acknowledge the gift other than to take the choker from his hand, but she also didn't refuse to wear the thing. He backed out and awaited her in the bedroom. When at last she was dressed, she joined him. She glowed. The yellow brought out the delicacy of her skin and changed the color of her eyes to summer blue, which under the candlelight seemed more pure than the deepest ocean. His heart expanded. He didn't want to be at odds with Cassia. He held out his hand to her, and she accepted his clasp. "I'm forgiven?"

"For tonight."

With no choice other than to be content with that edict, he obeyed the rules his father-in-law had suggested, joining his guests in the ballroom. Spring blooms decorated the entire area. Light music was supplied by a trio of violinists seated at the end of the room. First on the floor, he joined with Lady Gerard for a reel and next with Nora for a country-dance, but the dancing was as informal as the buffet. His guests appeared to greatly enjoy the relaxed atmosphere. He also danced with Amelia, who had helped his wife with the whole setup. "Very good of you," he said, stiffly.

"And it's very good of you not to tell your wife about me."

He smiled cynically. "It's not for me to shatter her illusions."

"I don't think we can keep it secret much longer." She sighed. The woman was beautiful and gentle, and while he did have sympathy for her, she had broken society's rules. Mistresses didn't socialize with wives.

He passed her on to George, who had been lurking about. When the evening finally began to draw to an end, Sir Waldo and Lady Gerard wandered into the sitting room with Sir Robert and Lady Lacey for a rest and a gossip while many others in the same age bracket began to leave. When only his close circle remained, Adam strode over to the trio. "Play a waltz," he said, and he found his wife supervising the removal of the empty plates from the buffet table. He took her hand and led her onto the floor. "Tonight has been most enjoyable. Are you tired?"

"A little. But I wanted the night to be a success."

While he slow waltzed her around the floor, she momentarily rested her head on his shoulder. "Our guests appear to have enjoyed themselves."

"I would say so. It was a nice change from the usual

formality of these things. You have a way of making people feel comfortable, no doubt about it."

"I'm glad." She smiled at him.

"George escorted Amelia home."

"I didn't notice she had left. I was too busy organizing the clean up." She glanced around as if checking that Amelia had gone. "I don't know how I would have managed without her. We must buy her a nice gift to show our appreciation."

"What would you suggest?"

"You choose. You seem to be rather an expert at gift giving. The necklace was a lovely surprise. It was much admired. I'm not accustomed to being so lavishly decorated. Thank you, Adam."

He breathed out with relief, now knowing she did appreciate his gift. "So, am I forgiven for whatever I did to upset you?"

"A person should never be bribed to forgive transgressions. I'll forgive you because you asked."

His heart full, he took her hand and led her over to the seating area she had set up near the buffet table. The lights from the sitting room flowed from the opened doors. The Graces still sat with Cassia's parents. Lucien, Jeremy, and Bertie sat listening to the violins with Cornelia Gerard, who would leave when her parents did. Adam seated Cassia and sat beside her with the younger group.

"We were watching you dance," Cornelia said, smiling. "You look so sweet together. It's so wonderful that you found each other."

"It helps to have friends, of course." Lucien pushed his

thumbs in his waistcoat pockets and leaned back with a smirk on his face.

Cassia glanced at him enquiringly. "You mean George introducing us?"

"I think you will find that Lucien meant the episode in the feed shed," Bertie said, shooting a quick glance at Lord Walton. "He helped by shutting you both inside on the night of the Gerard's ball."

"What makes you say that?"

"He told me."

Cornelia's eyes rounded in astonishment. "Lucien locked the hay shed door? Our hay shed? On the night you disappeared? Is that where you were? I wondered why everyone was creeping around the next morning. But how strange. Surely you remember the trick of it, Adam?"

"What trick?" Cassia asked, her cheeks cold.

"The lever sticks. Sometimes the door even often locks itself, especially when someone has slammed it. Don't you remember, Adam? Jeremy and you were locked in there years ago. Papa showed you both the metal placket we keep on the lintel that you push through the crack to lift the bar."

"He tried everything." Cassia blinked with concentration. "He shook the door, he kicked the door. But he couldn't budge it."

"How strange." Cornelia stared at Adam, and then she stared at her hands. "It was too dark, I expect. If it had been daylight, he would have remembered. Oh, that's funny, really. And very fortunate, because it gave you both time to fall in love."

In the silence, Adam cleared his throat. "Exactly."

The silence expanded. Bertie stared off into the distance, Lucien began a tuneless whistle, and Jeremy looked ready to explode with laughter.

"It's not funny, Jeremy, and it was meant to be kept quiet. Shall we *not* share this story with anyone else?" Cassia rose to her feet.

"Of course not, but it is funny, though I quite see why it isn't funny to you."

Adam kept his tone to a low growl. "Let's toast to secrets." He caught the eye of the footman, who hurried over. "Champagne for everyone, please."

The dreaded repercussions hit him when he entered his bedroom later.

Cassia had never expected a love match. She had expected to marry George and live happily with him. She had expected to produce children and run her household efficiently. An all-encompassing love had never been on her agenda. Being locked in the hay shed with Adam and therefore obliged to marry him hadn't particularly ruffled her feathers. The night they had spent together had proven him to be a kind and courteous man who had respected her unprotected position.

Later, on her honeymoon, she had discovered the pleasures of the flesh with him, and she blessed his patience. An episode that may have been awkward with George had been an enjoyable experience with Adam. And now, hearing that he had deliberately compromised her so that he could have his own way had set her alight with fury.

He would be taught a lesson. No one bested Cassia and lived to laugh. After they went up to bed, at least he had the good sense not to lay a hand on her, fortunately, because her cheeks were wet and she couldn't find the will to stop the flow. Not only was she humiliated, but every bone in her body ached. He had treated her like a chattel, not a person, and everyone knew. She had revered him for every possible wrong reason. Far from being honorable, the man was a disgraceful cad.

As soon as he left for his club in the morning, she ordered the carriage. She wasn't the only woman needing to escape a man.

"Here's what we will do," she said when Amelia opened the door to her. "We will run away together."

Amelia blinked. "That sweet of you, but you can't leave the duke because I am a fool."

"I'm a fool as well." Cassia marched into the sitting room and plumped down in the weary couch. "Did you know Adam tricked me into marriage?"

Amelia slowly shook her head.

"Damn his rotten soul. We had no need to stay in the horrible draughty shed all night. All the time he knew how to get out."

"What shed?"

"I went for a walk on the night of the Gerard's ball and the rain caught me by surprise. I ran into the feed shed. He ran in after me. The door slammed and we, I, couldn't open it. And he stayed with me all night so that he could have his way."

"He didn't." Amelia widened her eyes with shock.

"Not in that sense, no. He had said before that he

would marry me if I asked him. I expect vanity got the better of when I didn't. So he must have decided that if he compromised me, I would have to agree." Cassia crossed her arms over her chest.

"Don't you think that's rather flattering?"

"It is not. It's disgraceful. How can he imagine I will ever respect him after this?" Cassia's bottom lip wanted to quiver, but she would not lose control.

Amelia sat beside her on the sofa. "Did you expect to love him when you married him?"

"Heavens, no. Mind you, I found him attractive, especially that night, well, really from the first time I met him, but I was appalled that he had a mistress. George told me that."

"I wonder why?" Amelia's eyebrows drew together. "Was George trying to put you off the duke, or was he trying to tell you something?"

"I thought he was simply stating a fact. So, from then on, I tried to ignore Adam, but he is not easy to ignore, and we got off on the wrong foot with each other. When we were in the shed, he told me how awful and managing I was, and I told him he was disreputable and no decent woman would have him."

Amelia glanced away. "You don't mince words, either of you, do you?" Her lips quivered.

Cassia made an impatient gesture with her hand. "We had no need. Neither of us was trying to charm the other. But somehow we made peace. He was so incredibly patient. But that isn't to the point. He had no right to compromise me."

"Did you really want to marry George?" Amelia held her glance.

"I thought I did, but I might have come around if Adam had continued to court me. At times, he was charming and he could make me laugh. I like that in a man. And he never fusses with me. He leaves me to make my own decisions. He never minds what I do and he wouldn't think of giving me an order." Cassia's voice trembled. She drew her handkerchief out of her sleeve and blew her nose. "We work together well. And I wouldn't have known that if I hadn't been locked in the shed with him."

"So, all's well that ends well." Amelia's voice still held a tone of amusement.

"You can't imagine that I will take this controlling behavior lightly? It's not funny, Amelia."

"I know. But you needn't run away with me. You could probably poison his food instead."

"Trust me, I thought of that. But it would be awful if he died. I'm not completely sure I wouldn't miss him." Cassia blotted her eyes. "But he must be seeing his mistress again. He didn't mind at all when I turned my back on him last night."

"In that case, you have every right to assume he is seeing another woman. I quite agree. You ought to leave him. That would serve him right. Men should always mind when women are clearly showing their displeasure."

Cassia's lips trembled into a half smile. "Do you think your lover will worry when you leave?"

Amelia nodded, her expression growing more sober. "My hope is that he will miss me enough to be his own man and marry where his heart takes him."

Cassia clasped Amelia's hands. "I pray that happens. If you are forced to disappear because of the baby, I will lose the only real friend I have. I don't want to be selfish about losing you, but I have a plan that I took the whole night to organize in my head. First, I thought we should go to the Huntsdale country estate."

"You would be spotted there as quick as a wink."

"I know. And it's no good me hiring a coach because I would be caught out there, too," Cassia said with a certain amount of bitterness. "I think we need to hide in plain sight."

"But Cassia, I don't want to be in plain sight. I'm not running away to be found. I'm leaving so that I won't embarrass George. There, I have said his name." Amelia stared straight at Cassia, her expression combining defiance and shame. "I was the father's housekeeper in his father's town house until two months ago."

For a moment, Cassia sat as still as a statue, scarcely breathing. Her mind whirled. George. The last person she expected, though after the news of his other baby, perhaps she had been a little naïve. She drew a deep breath. "Well. Well, I'm glad someone as wonderful as you love him. He needs redeeming. That is what we shall try for. I can't see a single reason why his father should object to you, especially as he already knows you."

"I have the idea he wanted you for his son."

Cassia swallowed. Apparently, she had been the person who had blighted Amelia's life. Therefore, she should be the person who rectified the matter. "I really have no need to run away or hide, do I? I'm being quite pathetic. It's you who needs help. Well ... Papa and Nora are leaving for

Surrey in a few hours. Perhaps you ought to go with them."

Amelia blinked. "Do they need a housekeeper?"

"No, they need a house guest who ought to be seen by Mr. Penrose. If you are an honored guest, he is bound to think of you another way."

"Would your father take me as a guest?"

"I won't tell him why, of course, but he seemed to think you were a good friend for me last night. You won't be showing for a few months, and I'm sure we can cobble together a story for Papa so that he supports you. And Nora would certainly love your company if you help her with the boys. She would also like someone around who can run a house without trying to organize her, as I do. The more I think about this, the more I love the whole idea. Meanwhile, I will be in the city watching George fall apart because you have gone, and he doesn't know where." Cassia crossed her arms and managed a firm smile.

"I should protest ..." Amelia said uncertainly.

Cassia frowned. "Do you see a hole in my plan?"

"The only holey part might be if George doesn't miss me."

"Therefore, you have nothing to lose. You were planning to leave him. This way we, if we manage this, will get you married to him, which means you will be my friend forevermore, which is exactly what I want." But thoughts flowed through Cassia's head about all the times George had had walked or talked or danced with Amelia. He hadn't been acting the gentleman. He had been protecting her, while all the time he was the one who had put her in peril of others not doing the same. "Oh, dear. Now I wish I hadn't told you about his other baby. Why, oh why did I do so?"

"You weren't to know. At least you prepared me for my disillusionment."

"He told you he wouldn't marry you, didn't he?"

Amelia slowly shook her head. "I didn't tell him about my predicament. I didn't know what he would say, and if he rejected me, I would fall apart. Better that I leave before he has the chance."

"He hasn't refused to acknowledge you in public, though. That's a good sign, isn't it?"

"He has acknowledged me, but nothing more. He had to, since many of his friends knew me as the housekeeper. None has mentioned that, which is enormously kind of them. They pretend they have only met me recently as a friend of yours. I thought he loved me, but after you told me about the other woman, I saw him with different eyes. He could have barely been done with her before he set me up in my house."

Cassia let out a regretful breath. "Mistresses should not fall in love with the men who set them up."

"Is that a rule?"

"According to my husband, men make agreements with their mistresses."

"What do you mean?"

"I don't really know, but his agreed that no emotions should be involved in their relationship."

"He told you that?"

Cassia nodded. "I didn't ask for the information. He wanted to let me know that he wouldn't keep a mistress and a wife at the same time."

"Cassia, you are an incredible woman." Amelia laughed. "Is there nothing you won't discuss?"

"Hm. My limit hasn't been tested yet."

Amelia hugged her. "Well, I think your plan is wonderful. Now we only have to hope that your father will take me with them."

"George deserves that you should give him a great fright. You have been too patient with him."

"It seemed to me that if we had a chance to be alone together, he would see me as a woman rather than a rather exciting escapade."

"He's awfully irresponsible, Amelia. Can you bear that?"

"He's never had a need to be otherwise. The duke had to take over because his father died. George, until now, has had no need to do a thing but be a rich man's heir. He's certainly taking his job seriously. With luck, if he misses me, he will take our relationship more seriously, too."

Cassia rose to her feet. "Pack your bags. We can do this. I'll insist Papa use Adam's large carriage. He will adore that. It's the latest thing, and far more comfortable than his old contraption. He could even put the boys and the nanny in that one and have a much more comfortable trip. I must go, Amelia, to get this organized. Pack and don't say a word to your maid. Just leave with your bags when the carriage arrives." Cassia threw her arms around her friend and kissed her on the cheek. "I'll write to you and let you know what is happening in the city."

She sped back home to speak with her father and Nora, but she knew neither would mind having a friend of hers in the house, one who could help Nora. She told a quick, abbreviated story about poor widowed Amelia being Mr. Penrose's former housekeeper who had been employed in that manner, but would prefer to be a ladies' companion, but who first needed a short break. Nora would sympathize with another widow.

Nora gave Cassia an ecstatic hug when the idea was put to her. "She did such a wonderful job helping you for the spring party. I hope she won't mind helping me to organize something similar in Surrey. I never have arranged a function without you, you know."

"Make sure you invite Mr. Penrose, won't you? She would like him to see her in another setting."

Praying she would be up to the role of a devious woman, Cassia waved Adam's new carriage off, already satisfied with her machinations. The boys were pleased to be travelling, supervised only by a maid who indulged their every whim. All's well that ends well, as Amelia had said.

Adam merely nodded when she told him where his carriage had gone. "We don't need it at the moment. I wish you would tell me before you reorganize my household."

"You would be very bored if I did. I reorganize at least four things per day."

He stood gazing at her for a moment, and when she retained her cool expression, he drew a heavy sigh and made for his study.

Adam was pleased to hear that Amelia had left London, fortunately, before his wife discovered that the woman was George's mistress. Cassia would have been humiliated had she known. In her eyes, George was perfect. Although Adam would like to have been able to inform her otherwise, he didn't have the heart. He couldn't bear to see his trusting wife disillusioned. Best that the woman simply disappeared. Aside from that, he saw no need to be a righteous hypocrite.

However, his home life didn't take a turn for the better after Amelia went. He was still a rotting fish in his wife's eyes. No sooner had the Lacey family left than Cassia put the housemaids to a frenzy of cleaning, and herself to furious social activity. During the week, Cassia no longer sat with him in the evenings while he caught up on his paperwork. Instead, she attended every function known to man or beast. If Adam was otherwise engaged, she didn't appear bereft. She managed either with one of his friends or with the Graces.

The relationship he'd had with his wife turned into one of quick meetings and careful words. Although he had never taken lightly the fact that she hadn't married him because she loved him, he found his life no longer consisted of thought-sharing, interesting conversations, and bed sports. He now had an efficient arrangement, no more, no less. She never discussed where she had been or what she did. If he asked, she would tell him, but she appeared to no longer needed him in her world.

She hadn't moved out of his bedroom, but he wasn't blind, deaf, or dumb. If he attempted to take her into his arms, she would be a dutiful wife, but he didn't want a dutiful wife.

He wanted more.

However, his pride would not allow him to beg. She needed to see that she needed him the same way he needed her. In time, she would. He was an influential man who would spare no expense where she was concerned. And tonight, he lay with his arms behind his head. She had presented her back to him, *yet again*.

He tried *yet again*, by offering her what she may have wanted. "Normally I wait until parliament is in recess before I go to Kent, but I think we will go early this year ... perhaps in a day or two."

"I think *you* should, if you wish, but I have too much to do here, parties to attend, meetings of the Fumble Fingers—"

"Fumble Fingers?"

"That's what we call our gossip group when we sew for charity."

"The other members will be going to the country. The Gerards always do."

"George will be staying." Her tone sounded superior.

He sat up, staring down at the blonde head, which was his only vision of her. "George is not your husband."

"He is a very convenient substitute when I need a dancing partner or someone to talk to at a dinner."

"You don't need a substitute."

She slowly rolled over onto her back. "Then I *want* a substitute. He doesn't disappear all the time. He is available."

"I don't want my wife seeing other men." He crossed his arms over his chest, hoping to appear adamant rather than completely nonplussed.

"I'm a good wife to you, Adam. I have your house running like clockwork, and your servants are now well-trained. Your brother is more stable, and he eats more than he drinks. If I am failing in my duty, you only need to let me know where, and I will change."

What could a man say? *You are failing in the making-love area.* He would never say that. He shouldn't have to resort to telling her how much he loved having her in his arms. How much he loved her soft laugh. How much he loved the former softness in her eyes, the softness when she looked at him that she had lost since she had discovered that he knew how to open the feed shed door. He knew, yes, but the lever had been missing and the lock had rusted. None of that was Lucien's fault. He thought he was doing Adam a favor.

"You don't need to change for me," he said, sliding down in the sheets and managing to turn his back on her before she turned hers on him.

Chapter Fifteen

Cassia eased in beside George, who stood propping up a doorway in Mr. Arnold Walton's ballroom. Mr. Walton, Lucien's cousin, was a politician who enjoyed entertaining, which he did well. Couples had taken to the floor, but George hadn't danced all night. "I don't know why you come to these affairs, George, if you are not interested in young ladies."

"Habit. I'm supposed to be looking for a worthy aspirant to my hand, according to my father."

"I understand. You have seen how happy Adam is as a married man and you wish to follow suit."

George eyed her. "It's my father's idea, not mine."

"Let me help. Miss Havers currently has no partner. She would suit your father nicely. Not only is she beautiful, she excels in household management. She would never bore you because she rarely speaks, but underneath that quiet exterior dwells a very sweet young lady. Your father would adore her."

"I'm not in the market for sweet young ladies," George said sourly. "Aside from that, Lucien wants her."

"Surely you have enough address to cut out Lucien?"

He narrowed his eyes. "Flattery will get you nowhere, Cassia, as you certainly know."

"Perhaps you have a yen for another lady?" She watched his face.

George's mouth expressed his dissatisfaction. "One whom my father would never approve."

"Well, then, that cuts her out. Never mind. Let me bring over Miss Matthews. Your father would approve of her, though she is no longer a debutant."

"Cassia, find a partner for someone else. A yen is a yen and can't be easily cast off."

"If I weren't the mistress of decorum, I would shake you, George Penrose. Do you love this other lady or not?"

He stared at her, his eyebrows lifting and creasing his forehead. Then his gaze wavered. "I do." He heaved a long sigh. "But rather than have me, she disappeared. I couldn't ask her to marry me because my father would cut me out of his will. There. Now you think nothing of me. I am controlled by my father's money." He folded his arms across his chest.

"I have known you my whole life, George. I know how your father controls you with money. Yet, you have all the right contacts, and you know you do. If your father threw you out, I'm quite sure your friends would rally around and you would have another place in a trice. Perhaps, for a time, you could no longer be a gentleman of leisure, but you know you are your father's only heir and he loves you. He also wants what is best for you. His problem is that he doesn't understand that love in a marriage is important. You do. I have discovered that I do, too." She drew a deep breath. "If you truly loved this lady, you should defy your father. He will surely come around."

He sighed. "Believe me, I have had everyone of those thoughts, but I have searched London and I can't find her. I've checked hotels and post houses, but she could be anywhere. I simply don't know where to look."

"If you found her, would you ask for her hand in marriage?"

"I believe that's the only way I could keep her. She has shown me clearly that without marriage she will not stay."

"In that case, my dear friend, I believe I can help you if the lady's name is Amelia."

He stared at her, his mouth slack. Then his eyes narrowed with suspicion. "You wretch," he said under his breath. "You have known about us all along. I ought to have realized because you have spent your life interfering in mine. Why I put up with you ..." A smile slowly broke out on his face. He grabbed both her hands and kissed one. "And this is why. You understand what true friendship is."

She glanced around, her own smile demure. Adam's blazing gaze hit her from across the room. The stark blue glitter in his eyes expressed his dangerous thoughts. The man had a jealous streak a mile wide. Normally, she wouldn't stoop to subterfuge, but she'd recently had the lowering thought that, despite the fact that he had forced her marriage to him, if he would only tell her he loved her, she might be tempted to forgive him. She certainly enjoyed being his wife. The 'fors' outweighed the 'againsts' but a woman with any pride wouldn't allow him to get away with taking whatever he wanted without suffering a consequence or two.

She stayed by George's side, her hand tucked beneath his arm, her doting smile not faltering. If Adam's less than admirable possessiveness caused him to stride across the room and snatch her into his arms, she would not mind a jot. A show of affection for her would do much to elevate her spirits. However, the self-contained man who had decided he would marry her whether she wanted him or not, disliked showing his feelings.

Lately, she had begun to suspect that he might be trying to buy her affection. When she pleased him, he showed his appreciation by giving her expensive jewelry. Since the day two weeks ago when she had discovered he had kept her locked in the hayshed, she had begun to suspect that, when he had told her he would marry her if she asked, he already had he had a fondness for her. Either that, or he wouldn't allow himself to be thwarted.

She glanced at the polished floorboards rather than at her obstinate husband. On her honeymoon, she had enjoyed the autocrat's company. She had certainly enjoyed her wedding night, and the following week in the country as she grew to know him. By then, he understood her well enough to see that she needed no supervision. Only a rare and strong man could manage that. Unlike many other husbands, he didn't see the need to interfere with her decisions or make sure she adhered to his budget, or didn't hire too many servants, or make a wilderness of his garden. He had trusted her with his house and his servants, unlike her father who constantly checked her every deed.

Trust and love came together. She had trusted Adam, but he hadn't been truthful with her. His betrayal had honestly hurt. Now she had virtually estranged herself from him. She missed the warmth of his companionship. If she tested him and he failed, her heart might ache, but she would lose nothing. She had come into the marriage merely expecting him to respect her, as she planned to respect him, but her fascination had turned into love. When, how, or why, she didn't know.

However, a marriage in which only one partner loved would never be as satisfying as one in which two partners loved. Few people expected more out of marriage. Being largely uncommunicative, he didn't need to gush, but sometimes when he glanced at her, she thought she noted a strange softness in his eyes. But words were important too. She drew a deep breath, turning her face away from George to speak, hoping to appear furtive. "In fact, I can take you to her, if you call for me in the morning around half-past eight. You will need a travelling carriage, for we will have quite a trip." Then she glanced up at him, hoping that her lash fluttering would make her appear doting to any husband who happened to be watching.

He stared guardedly at her. "Quite a trip? I use my curricle for long distance driving."

"That won't do at all. You would expose me to the weather. You could use your barouche if you wish."

"Why not just tell me where she is and I can go alone?"

"Do you want to see her or not?" She tried a pretty

pout, which George would never notice was faked. He expected that from women. "If you don't take me, the whole thing will blow up in your face. Pack a trunk. And don't say a word to Adam."

"*Or if I do, I won't see Amelia*. Yes, I understand. You don't want Adam to know about this, though how you can gallivant about the place with me all day without him being extremely annoyed with you, I can't imagine. On your head be it. If he confronts me, I will confess that the idea was all yours."

She laughed. "Tattletale." Her heart thumped. Dare she do this? She dropped her hold on his arm and joined the group of ladies she knew best until Rodney Toddington asked her to dance.

Then Adam decided they needed to leave early. He barely spoke to her in the carriage, which suited her. Elsie had waited up to undress her, which caused Cassia a modicum of guilt. Had she been on better terms with Adam, her maid could have had an early night. "I'll brush my own hair, Elsie, and you must go. But I will want you early in the morning for I have a special task for you. Goodnight."

Adam slept with his back to her. She lay awake for quite a while, plotting.

As usual, Adam arose early and didn't wake her, which didn't matter because she barely slept. She slipped out of bed and began to pack a small trunk. Elsie arrived and dressed Cassia in a heavy cotton gown, as requested. "Now, Elsie, the task. Put one gown in the trunk for me, and night attire. I don't plan to be away for any length of time." She drew a breath. "And I need to ask a favor of you."

Elsie straightened. "Yes, your grace."

"I won't tell you what I plan to do so that you don't have to lie for me. I simply want you to do as I ask."

"I don't mind lying for your grace."

"Perhaps not." Cassia smiled. "But my husband could take offense and we don't want that. You are helping me to pack and I haven't told you where I am going. You could be rather suspicious when you wander to the window and see me step into Mr. George Penrose's barouche at about eight-thirty. You could even be slightly worried because I seemed secretive while you were packing for me. And no one would blame you if you mentioned your perplexity to Mr. Jeremy when he appears for breakfast later."

"How much later?" Elsie asked, not meeting Cassia's gaze.

"As late as possible. If he lingers over his breakfast and newspaper until ten, that would be most convenient."

"Yes, your grace." Elsie aimed her smile at the carpet.

Huntsdale lifted his gaze from his newspaper. Recently, he had spent his mornings at Whites, discussing the latest political shenanigans. Anywhere was better than at home. At home, he couldn't bear to see his wife in a mope about another man. He wanted to explain George's unworthiness, and the reason for Adam's inability to let Lucien take the blame for the door being stuck. He wanted to ask for her forgiveness, but if he did, he had to tell a woman who didn't love him, that he loved her.

Yes, he loved her.

He loved her to the depths of his being, but if she didn't feel the same way, he would understand exactly why his father had nothing but bitter words for his mother. Saving his words spared him that, at least. A shadow appeared in front of him. He glanced up at his brother.

"I don't know whether to disturb you with this or not," Jeremy said, his face creased. "You may know something I don't. Was Cassia planning a long trip today?"

"I don't ask her to tell me what she plans to do."

"She took a packed trunk with her."

Adam's heartbeat tripped, but he managed a casual shrug. "Her ladies collect clothes for the poor. I'm sure you know that."

"I do, but Elsie was worried about her mistress and she told me she packed the duchess's gowns for a stay somewhere. She didn't tell Elsie where, and Elsie saw her step into George's barouche right after you left for here. He also had a packed trunk in the barouche."

"Perhaps he is taking her home to Surrey."

"And she didn't tell you? Why wouldn't she? Aside from that, her parents have barely left London. But if you don't care what your wife is doing, then why should I?" Jeremy shot an accusing glare at Huntsdale.

The world outside appeared to rock. Adam clung to the arms of his chair. "Indeed. Why should you?"

After holding an unconcerned expression on his face while waiting for the interminable time for Jeremy to turn on his heel and leave, Adam hurried outside and hailed the first cab that passed. His mind raced from one explanation to another. Cassia had planned a visit to her parents. Her parents had barely left his house. She would never be so unmannerly as to leave him without a word.

Of course she would.

Last night, she had flirted quite openly with George.

The signs had been there for weeks. She didn't want him. She was no longer interested in married congress with him since she had discovered from Bertie's ill-advised words that she hadn't been accidentally compromised at all. If he had known what Lucien had done … but he hadn't. The situation couldn't have been changed, no matter what.

In the beginning of their marriage, she had not been averse to him. She had never slapped his hands off her. After marriage, she had been a more than willing virgin sacrificed to the altar of his lust. He should have found the words to tell her long since, that he had wanted her since the day they had met. Only his fear of her scorn had stopped him.

As the hansom clipped to his house, he noticed that his hands shook. He wondered in which direction George would have taken Cassia. Where could they go? George wouldn't install her as his mistress. Society would be outraged and he would not be able to show his face in England for years. George would never cope with that.

Within five minutes Adam leapt out of the cab at the front of his house, knowing he had to find the couple before too long a time passed. He would try for forgiveness; a second chance. He would give her rubies. She seemed to prefer the colored stones to diamonds. Last night, she had worn the pearl and peridot necklace again, and he recalled the secret smile on her face while George whispered sweet nothings in her ear.

The thought of Cassia loving anyone but him expanded

an aching void inside his chest. He took the path to the mews, his skin icy cold. "Are you there, Matt?" he called.

The head coachman stepped out of the stables. "Yes, me Lord Duke. Was you wanting a carriage?"

"I'll have the curricle readied within five minutes."

The coachman rubbed his chin. "Can't be done. We 'aven't had that out in a month of Sundays. We would 'ave to clean it up before you use it."

"Hitch up my chestnuts. I'll give you five minutes while I change. By the way, did you see my wife leave this morning?"

The man stared. "No sir, but the footman 'anded 'er up."

"And ...?"

"'e was somewhat of the opinion that Mr. Penrose looked a trifle frazzled." Matt took a step back and stared above Adam's head.

Adam turned on his heel and entered the house from the back. He strode to the front and found the footman refilling the night lamps. "Did my wife give you a message for me this morning when she left?"

The footman shook his head. "She said nothing to me, your grace, but she asked Mr. Penrose how long he imagined it would take him to drive to Surrey. I took note, because I was not aware she was leaving. Looked proper worried, too, she did. *Oh, we must be there before nightfall*, she said. I take it that she had news of something amiss at home." The footman raised his eyebrows, his face clearly expressing doubt.

Adam nodded and dashed up the stairs. He shouldn't imagine that his wife had run off with her old flame. She would be off to see to her father or her stepmother or one of the boys. He would find a message waiting for him in the bedroom.

But he didn't, *as he knew he wouldn't.*

Refusing to experience a single emotion, with shaking hands, he donned his driving coat and made sure his wallet was full. He could travel faster with two horses changed at every post than George could ever manage with those slugs of his pulling his barouche. At least Adam knew in which direction to go now.

Was George lost to all morality? Did he assume his father would take in a married lady who certainly wouldn't be given a divorce by her husband. Ever. Or was George taking her to her own parents? Why? She could take herself, if it came to that. Regardless, Adam couldn't let his wife leave him without her explaining herself.

While he remained in the city precincts, he kept his horses tightly reigned. As soon as he reached the outskirts, he urged his team into a gallop. His heart beat kept time with the pounding hooves. George had an hour's head start on him. Huntsdale would make up an hour and possibly run down the couple before they reached their destination. They might take their time, not expecting Huntsdale to give chase.

He wondered where George kept his brain. Somewhere lower than his head, clearly. George had surely guessed that Adam had feelings for Cassia, and George knew that Adam didn't easily give up. Barely restraining his ruptured thoughts, he whistled the whip in the air above the horses' heads.

When he spotted the first post-house, he drew up his

lathered team. The fresh horses fought the bit but finally gave in after snorting and tossing their heads, reminding Adam of his courtship. Cassia had not accepted his first tentative proposal. She'd had to be compromised to do so. The moment she found out that the locking of the door had been no accident, she had raced off, which the nags were now doing, finding the chaise lighter than perhaps expected.

The amount of potholes in the road forced him to rein to a trot. Impatience caused sweat to pool beneath his hat. In a flurry of dust, he passed by empty paddocks and fields ready for harvesting. The road ahead interested him more than any scenic view.

The last time he had travelled this way was the day he had met Cassia at the picnic in Surrey. A crowd of his friends had filled his carriage. Picnic baskets had been piled on top. They had started early and hadn't hurried. If he had known he would meet his future wife, he may have been as urgent as he was today. As he began to think again of the impulsive woman he had married, he noticed a barouche ahead. He held his breath as he neared.

When he recognized that the carriage was indeed George's barouche, he released his pent-up tension with a shout. The driver's black hat bobbed along with the ruts in the road. Adam could barely pass. His wheels missed the others by inches while he called for the driver to stop. Whether or not the man recognized him was debatable, but he had no choice other than to pull up the barouche, for Adam crossed in right front of him.

His mind dazed, Adam tied the reins to the brake and stepped down, clenching his whip in one hand as he strode to the other man's carriage. The door opened. George's head appeared. "Good God. It's Adam." He fell back onto his seat, blinking.

Cassia appeared in the doorframe, staring at her shaken husband. "I didn't expect to see you here." She offered him lifted eyebrows.

With one foot on the step, he extended his arm. "I have come to take you home, my dear," he said through his gritted teeth.

"How kind, but I was planning to go on." She sat back in the carriage, her expression contumacious.

"Not with George, you're not." He stood his ground.

Her stubborn chin lifted. "He needs me."

"You married me."

"Oh, *you need me*, do you? Are the servants misbehaving? Are the meals atrocious? What could the problem possibly be?" She folded her arms.

"Are you insane, woman? You can't run off with my friends the moment the impulse takes."

She shrugged. "It can't make a jot of difference to you. You've had what you wanted out of me. You have a gracious home that now runs well with the right servants. You have meals delicious enough to impress your friends. Tell the driver to start up, George."

Adam glanced at George. "Do so, and I will drag you out of that carriage by your collar and the seat of your breeches."

George glanced at his fingernails. "I take it you want your wife back?"

"She failed to ask my permission to leave."

George lifted his eyebrows and stared at Cassia with an

annoyingly casual expression on his face. "Ask him, Cassia, and then we can be on our way."

"I don't think I need his permission to leave." Her chin lifted even higher. "We shall proceed on our journey."

Adam grasped the barouche door as if he could stop the departure with his bare hands. "Cassia, you shall not leave me."

Cassia drew a breath, her gaze on his. "I've yet to hear a good reason why I shouldn't."

"You're my wife." He squared his jaw, not about to move in this lifetime.

Cassia sighed loudly and glanced out the opposite side.

George pasted a smile on his face, lifting his hands. "I think that's settled, Adam. If you don't mind, we'll be on our way." He lurched back as Adam took the step into the carriage. "Unless, of course, you decide to speak civilly to your wife. I've known her long enough to be quite sure she is not used to being told what she will do, or that she needs your permission to—"

"—run away with you," Adam said harshly, finishing the sentence for him. "I suspect she doesn't. I suspect when a woman wishes to bolt, she does so without her husband's permission. Cassia, we should discuss this. You have no need to be so hasty. I'm sorry I, er ..."

She turned her gaze back to him and tilted her eyebrows. "Imprisoned me in the feed shed? Doing so was quite unnecessary, don't you think?"

His breath came more shallowly. His eyes ached. He rubbed the area where his heart continued to beat frantically. "I had no other choice."

"And so I thought, until I discovered the truth. You

could have let me out. No woman wants to look foolish, and that's what eventuated. You could have any amount of women. You didn't need to prove a thing to me."

"But I couldn't let you out, Cassia." His voice caught in his throat. "The lever was missing and I don't want any amount of women. I want you."

She gazed at her lap while George fidgeted. "Why?" she asked, her tone expressionless.

"I don't know."

George exhaled loudly. "I can't believe I befriended such a thickhead."

Adam stared at him, frowning, and then his jaw loosened. "Well, of course I love her, you raving fool. Why else would I be here? I can't lose her to you."

George offered him an open hand gesture. "Carry on, man. Speak to your wife, not me."

Adam's throat constricted. "I love you, Cassia," he said huskily. "I am glad the lever was missing because without you, I have no life, simply an existence." His chest filled with an ache that wouldn't leave. He met her glance. "May I have another chance to prove myself to you?"

She took her time perusing his face. Then, expressionless, she pursed her lips and leaned forward to speak to George. "First, you must go to your father, George, and explain about Amelia. Then you will find Amelia at my father's house. The rest is up to you. I shall now leave with my husband. Best of luck, my dear friend." She stood and kissed George on the cheek.

Adam backed out of the carriage and caught Cassia as she followed. He placed her carefully on the ground but left his hands on her waist, hoping to hear words of forgiveness.

She placed her hands on his shoulders. "Tell me again."

He breathed out. "Without you, I have no life."

"The other part."

"About giving me a chance?" He stared deep into her beautiful eyes, not sure what he saw there other than a question.

"Close, but no cigar." George's voice came from the carriage. He pulled shut the door and called to the driver to proceed. The barouche rumbled off, leaving a drift of dust in the wake.

Adam took Cassia's hands in his, and spoke the words he had never said to another living being. "I love you." He held his breath.

She stood, her gaze settling on his shirt-front. "Would you really have dragged George out of the coach?" Her lashes shaded her expression.

"Of course."

A tiny smile reached her mouth. "He didn't seem to be afraid."

"He knew that despite my fury, I wouldn't kill him." He lifted one of her hands and placed a kiss on the knuckles of her glove.

"You've fought with him before?" She dragged in a huge breath.

"Of course." He had no idea how to convey to Cassia how much he loved her. She certainly wasn't about to let him kiss her and show her instead. Not being an orator, he believed actions spoke louder than words. Cassia had clearly not realized that every time he made love to her, he added his heart and his soul. He could do no more. "Was I wrong? Were you running off with George or not?"

"I was running off with him," she said promptly. She stared off into the paddocks.

He narrowed his eyes. "And yet you were telling him where to find Amelia."

"He needed a second option if he couldn't have me."

He placed his forefinger along the side of her jaw to encourage her to look up at him. A lightness formed in his chest, and his mouth relaxed. "You have a glib but unconvincing tongue, my beautiful icicle. I believe you love me, too. When we give each other pleasure, I could swear don't object to me."

"I don't object to *that*. You're a skilled lover. You are experienced."

"I'm not experienced in telling anyone that I love her, even my own precious wife. I have only said those words once before, and that was today under duress of losing the woman I love." He swallowed. "I shall repeat that I love you more than life itself, Cassia. I love that you don't need me to tell you how to run my house. I love your independence. I love the fragrance of your hair. I love the way you fit into my arms."

She placed her palms against his chest and smiled shyly up at him. "I don't suppose we ever had time to speak words of love to each other. We had too much to do. I began to love you on our wedding night, but I couldn't be sure that I simply loved, hm."

"Sexual congress?"

"That, yes. Then I appreciated you didn't meddle. You let me do whatever I wished with the household and you were also free with your body."

His mouth ticked into a smile. "With making love?"

"Letting me explore your body." She dropped her gaze. "You trusted me with not only your possessions, but with yourself. But how could I say I loved you when you married me because you compromised me?"

"And how could I say I compromised you when I loved you? I thought you might do exactly as you did—run off." His fingers touched the back of her neck, and his thumb rested on the side of her jaw. He stayed focused on her eyes.

She turned up her face and he took her mouth slowly and gently, love expanding with his every breath. Her arms encircled his neck. Never in his life had he experienced a kiss so sweet. Without a doubt, the kiss could change within an instant to one of passion, but a dusty road, with two hired horses trying to edge his curricle over the verge to tear off strands of grass, was no place for a man to make love to his wife. "Though you weren't really running from me, were you?" he whispered gently against her silky hair.

Her laugh came soft and low. "Merely hoping you would chase me. I had no more than one gown in my trunk, and I think I forgot my hairbrush. Still, my plan worked. You confessed all to me, and best of all, you worked out that you love me. What more could I ask from a hastily contrived plan?"

"I think you also put your friend and her lover together, too."

"I had no choice. I don't like losing friends and I would have had to get rid of George if he hadn't confessed he loved Amelia."

With his palm on her back, he turned her toward the curricle. "I had no idea you were so ruthless, my love. Fortunately for me, my only sin was one of omission."

She stepped up while he walked the horse around a half circle, ready to head back home. "I do hope so. Running all over the countryside is rather tiresome. My, the weather is hot. Might we stop at the nearest tavern for a cool drink?"

"I suspect a light luncheon is in order as well. Whatever is the world coming to, when a man has to eat in a tavern with his very own absconding wife?"

Chapter Sixteen

Cassia and Adam arrived home in the late afternoon. Apparently, Elsie had performed her role to perfection. No one in the household suspected Cassia had disappeared. The servants were preparing for their own meal, which she had planned with the cook last week that would be served later for her and Adam. She hadn't arrived home with her trunk, which was on the way to Surrey with George. He would send her few belongings back. She shared her secret smile with her dressing room mirror as she removed her hat.

Adam loved her.

The foolish man should have said so long since. After having had a mistress, he should know the vagaries of females. How fortunate that he hadn't fallen in love with her. And how fortunate that George had fallen in love with his.

Adam didn't go back to his club. He decided he needed to sit at home with his wife. She changed into her green silk and had Elsie brush her hair into a twisted roll on her crown, not only the easiest hairdo, but the one that suited her best. Although after three months married to a duke had not, nor ever would, put her among the stylish matrons, at least she knew that the simpler the style she chose, the larger the compliment she received from her husband.

After a wonderful candlelit dinner, she was guided by Elsie to her dressing room and a steaming bath. "So exactly what I needed, Elsie. You are a marvel."

"Not me, ma'am. His grace said to make sure we had enough hot water tonight because as sure as eggs you would want a relaxing bath. What with travelling all over the place, you would be fair tired."

"I didn't travel too far, thanks to you." Cassia smiled. "You obeyed my instructions to the letter. I have something for you I think you might like." She stepped over to her jewelry box and considered for a moment, before bringing out a pearl brooch that wouldn't be too ostentatious for the young woman to wear. "I had this for my thirteenth birthday. I hope you like it."

"Thank you, ma'am. It's lovely," Elsie said shyly. "But I didn't help because I wanted a reward. I wanted you and the master to be happy. He needed waking up to himself, he did, and I was pleased to help."

"I'm very fortunate in you. Thank you, Elsie. And I won't need you again tonight."

Elsie tried to look suitably bland, but she giggled as she left the dressing room. Cassia gave a rueful smile, hoping that the household would not be regaled with the story of her racing off and then being brought back by her husband. Fortunately, she would never know. She undressed and sank back in the water, knowing she would sleep like the dead tonight.

Her husband had other ideas. He lit the room with candles, a very dangerous thing to do, but what could a woman say when a man insisted on being obvious? "Your subtlety leaves a lot to be desired," she said, disrobing and swinging her feet onto the bed.

"Do you want the room dark?"

She tried a demure face, but she had made love, without realizing she had been loving this man possibly a hundred times. He knew every inch of her body in the dark. "Not at all. I just don't want to start a fire."

"Ever practical Cassia. Perhaps you started a fire inside me."

"Ever romantic Adam."

"Do you think I'm romantic?"

She patted the bed beside her. "Yes, of course. This ..." She indicated the candlelit room. "And the way you give me gifts."

"What about the way I give you gifts?" He slid in beside her.

"Unexpectedly. Whenever you think I need one. I have something serious to tell you, Huntsdale."

He visibly tensed. "Go ahead."

She leaned over him and stared right into his eyes. "I love you."

He stared at her, his face aglow. "I love you too. I can't imagine my life without you." He snatched her into his arms and pressed his bristled cheek against hers. Then he began his wonderful kisses.

She had thought lovemaking was glorious before, but

making love to the man with whom she had pledged to worship with her body, or perhaps that had been his pledge, and possibly was because he did, was the most wondrous element of her marriage.

When she awoke early in the morning, she glanced at her tousle-headed husband's sleepy face.

He sat up, his expression slowly changing into indulgent amusement. "Have you ever been to the continent?"

She shook her head.

"This is all too much for me. I think we need a holiday."

"Perhaps. If we go away, I want you to treat me like your mistress."

"Trust me, you have a better bargain in being my wife."

"In the bedroom, Adam. I don't want a baby in the first year."

"Is that all you have to say?"

"I adore you, my delightful duke."

Also by Virginia Taylor

Spring of Love Series

Forever Delighted

Forever Amused

Forever Heartfelt

More from Serenade Publishing

Brigadier Station Series
By Sarah Williams:
The Brothers of Brigadier Station
The Sky over Brigadier Station
The Legacies of Brigadier Station
Christmas at Brigadier Station (An Outback Christmas Novella)
The Outback Governess (A Sweet Outback Novella)

Heart of the Hinterland Series
By Sarah Williams:
The Dairy Farmer's Daughter
Their Perfect Blend
Beyond the Barre

Primrose Series
By Tanya Renee
Prairie Sky

Prairie Nights

Prairie Fire

A New Page

by Aimee MacRae

It Happened in Paris

By Michelle Beesley

For more information visit:
www.serenadepublishing.com

About the Author

After training at the South Australian School of Art, Virginia accepted a job at an advertising agency. With a more interesting working life in mind, she retrained as a nurse, and then a midwife. By then, she met the man of her dreams, married, had two children, worked part time, and began writing romance.

www.ingramcontent.com/pod-product-compliance
Lightning Source LLC
Chambersburg PA
CBHW051421290426
44109CB00016B/1378